HALLOWEEN ORIGAMI

Nick Robinson

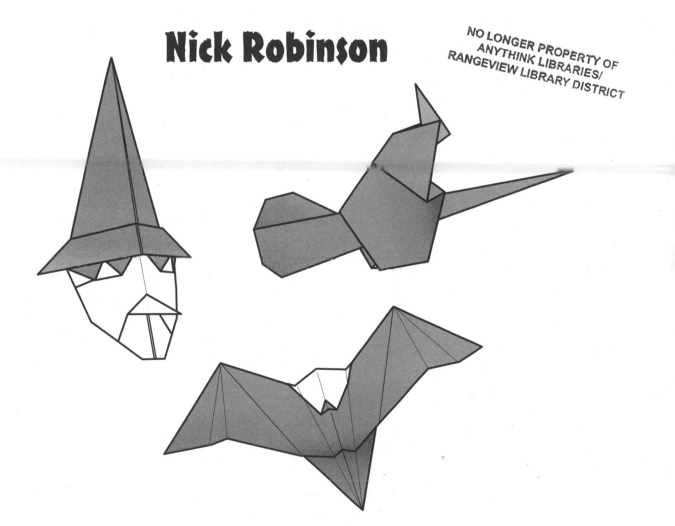

Dover Publications, Inc.

Mineola, New York

Bibliographical Note

Halloween Origami is a new work, first published by Dover
Publications, Inc., in 2012.

International Standard Book Number
ISBN-13: 978-0-486-49873-7
ISBN-10: 0-486-49873-5

Manufactured in the United States by Courier Corporation
49873501
www.doverpublications.com

Contents

Introduction

Origami is the art of folding paper to create models. These may be lifelike, abstract, or geometric forms. This book brings together a range of designs that reflect the theme of "Halloween." Since many of the subjects here are fantasy figures, the origami creator can exercise their imagination to try and capture the chosen subject.

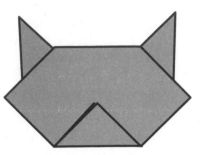

Despite what some people think, folding paper isn't something for which you need huge amounts of dexterity or skill. What you do need is a little patience and a desire to create something out of (almost) nothing. Origami is a form of magic—people will be amazed as you create a pair of vampire fangs or a flying witch in front of their eyes.

How to Fold

The keywords are "slowly" and "carefully"—try not to rush through a model (it will look rushed) and make sure every crease is as neat and accurate as you can make it. Anything less will result in a scruffy model and possibly even an incomplete model. Truly mastering origami can be a lifetime's study.

The act of folding is a motor skill that becomes easier with practice and concentration. Until it becomes second nature, make a deliberate effort to slow the process down. Don't be tempted to position the paper quickly, but move it in smaller and smaller increments until you are sure it is in the correct position. Hold the paper in position with one hand, then make the crease with the other. Then reinforce the crease, so it is crisp and the paper lies as flat as it can.

Where & When to Fold

Preparation is the key to an enjoyable folding experience. Find a perfectly flat table with plenty of space for you to arrange your instructions and spare paper. Always choose somewhere that is well lit. Try also to arrange for at least 30 minutes of uninterrupted time in which to concentrate—if you are in a hurry, your folding may well reflect this. Don't tackle new projects when you are tired and stressed and always use larger sheets of perfectly square paper—you can look at folding miniatures later on when you have mastered the design.

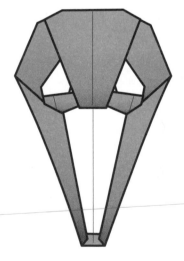

Using this Book

A range of folding techniques are used, with models ranging from the simple to the complex. You are advised to start by studying the section on symbols and bases—proper understanding of origami instructions will mean you can fold not only the models in this book, but those you find on the Internet, even when they are in a foreign language. Start the models at the beginning and work your way through, unless you're already a black belt in origami. Always read the associated text before attempting each step. It's also useful to look ahead at the next step, so you can see what you are aiming at.

If You're Struggling

As the designs become more advanced, you may find that you don't finish the model at the first attempt. At any point, if the paper is looking tired and crumpled, simply put it in the recycle bin and start over with a fresh sheet—each time you fold a model it will become easier and look neater. If perfection was easy to achieve, it wouldn't be worth striving for, so don't expect every model to look wonderful the first time you fold it.

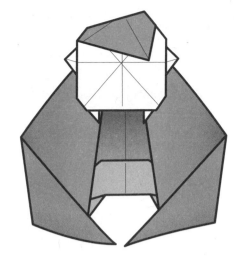

Folding in a group with other more experienced folders is highly recommended, since they will be able to quickly help you past those awkward steps and share their experiences (and models) with you. There are thousands of small origami groups around the world. Checking on the Internet will quickly track them down and they will be delighted to meet, help, and encourage you.

Paper

When learning a model, most types of thin paper will be OK, but make sure the sheet is on the large side. Once you have perfected the folding sequence, choosing the right type of paper can make a big difference to the finished result. More complicated designs may need thinner paper, others look better from slightly thicker paper.

Do you see both sides of the paper on the finished model? If so, try to find paper with suitable, complementary colors. Try to build up a collection of different types, colors, and patterns of paper, so you can use the perfect sheet for every model you make. Don't feel obliged to use dedicated origami paper—if you want a large model you will inevitably need to buy a very large rectangle or roll of paper and cut your own square (accurately!) from it.

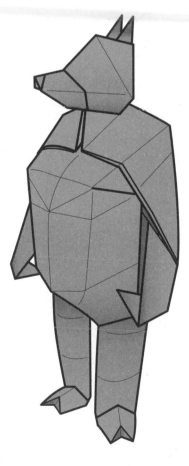

What's Next?

If you work through this book and find yourself wanting to fold more, welcome to the wonderful world of origami! Look on the Web for your Origami Society—in America it is Origami USA, in Great Britain it is the British Origami Society but there are many others around the world. Having found it, please join it—you will receive regular magazines, access to new models and exotic paper and most importantly, you will be part of a global community of folders.

Most importantly, enjoy yourself!

Nick Robinson

Folding Symbols

All origami instructions use a common set of symbols which allow you to make the model even if the words are a foreign language. On this page, these symbols are explained using an abstract design.

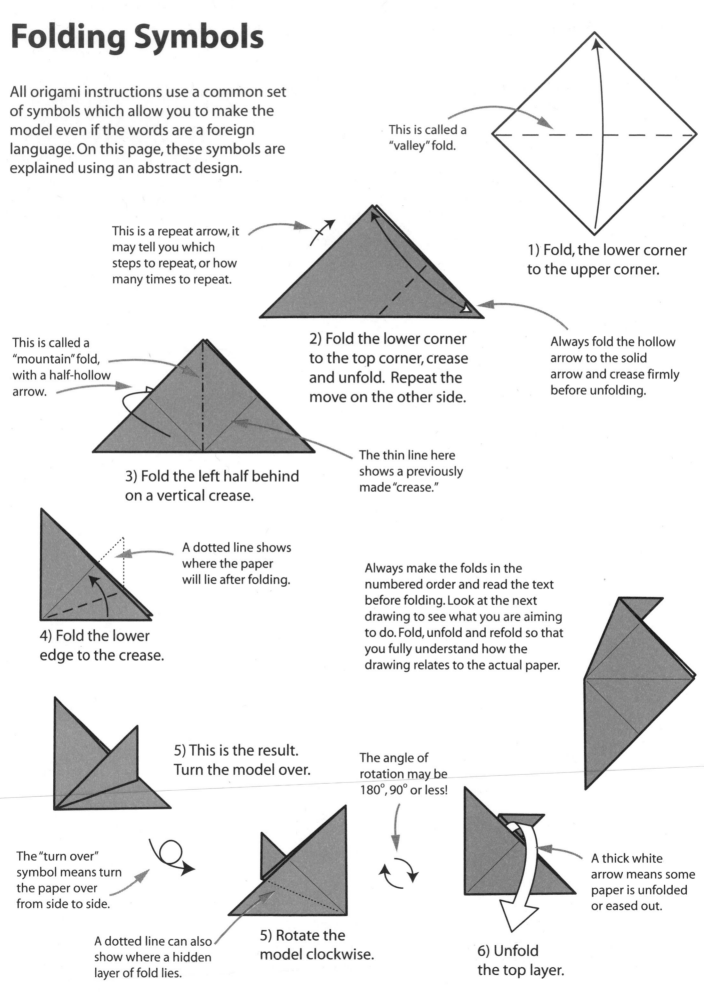

This is called a "valley" fold.

1) Fold, the lower corner to the upper corner.

This is a repeat arrow, it may tell you which steps to repeat, or how many times to repeat.

2) Fold the lower corner to the top corner, crease and unfold. Repeat the move on the other side.

Always fold the hollow arrow to the solid arrow and crease firmly before unfolding.

This is called a "mountain" fold, with a half-hollow arrow.

The thin line here shows a previously made "crease."

3) Fold the left half behind on a vertical crease.

A dotted line shows where the paper will lie after folding.

Always make the folds in the numbered order and read the text before folding. Look at the next drawing to see what you are aiming to do. Fold, unfold and refold so that you fully understand how the drawing relates to the actual paper.

4) Fold the lower edge to the crease.

5) This is the result. Turn the model over.

The angle of rotation may be 180°, 90° or less!

The "turn over" symbol means turn the paper over from side to side.

A dotted line can also show where a hidden layer of fold lies.

5) Rotate the model clockwise.

A thick white arrow means some paper is unfolded or eased out.

6) Unfold the top layer.

6

Other Techniques

You will find that some folding techniques are used very often and although they may vary slightly, are given names. When you see the name in the instructions, you can then draw upon your previous experience to complete the step.

outside reverse fold

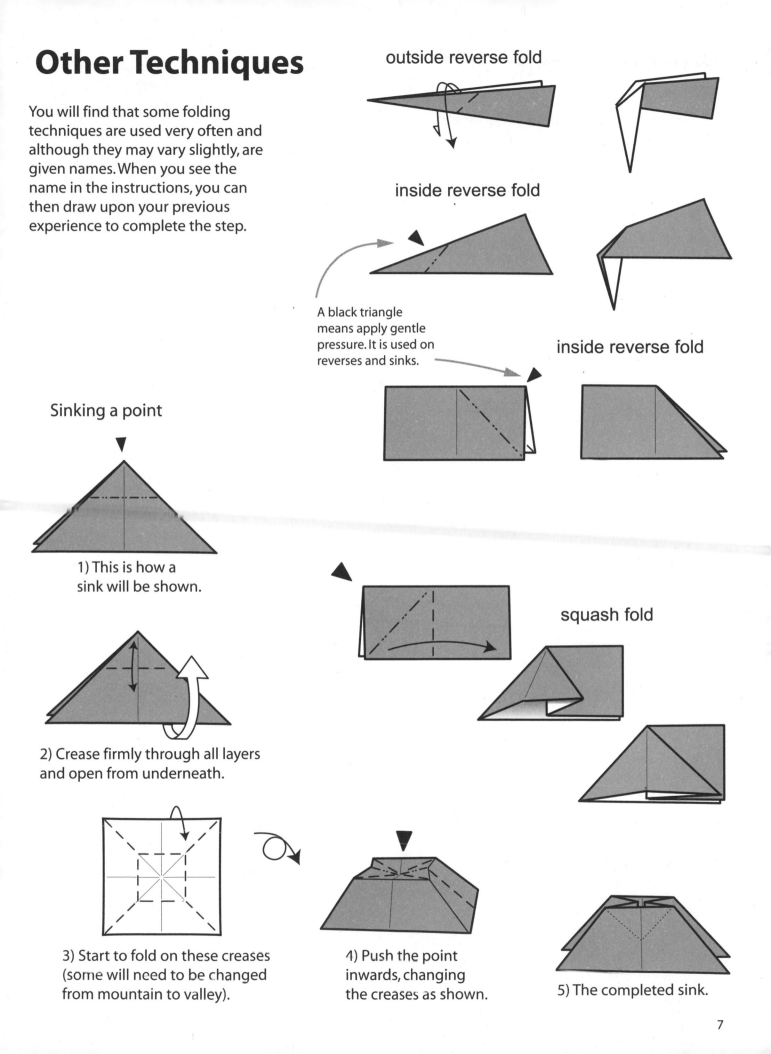

inside reverse fold

A black triangle means apply gentle pressure. It is used on reverses and sinks.

inside reverse fold

Sinking a point

1) This is how a sink will be shown.

2) Crease firmly through all layers and open from underneath.

squash fold

3) Start to fold on these creases (some will need to be changed from mountain to valley).

4) Push the point inwards, changing the creases as shown.

5) The completed sink.

Bases

Bases are simple folding sequences that are used in many origami models. Once you know them, you can often skip several steps of a diagram. They are also great ways to start creating your own designs.

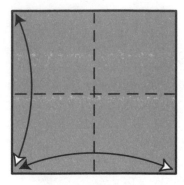

1) Fold in half and unfold, repeat in the other direction.

2) Turn over and crease both diagonals.

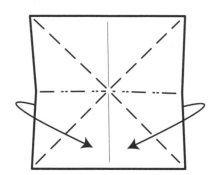

3) Collapse the paper down into a triangle.

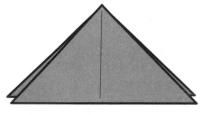

The waterbomb base

The preliminary base

1) Crease and unfold both diagonals.

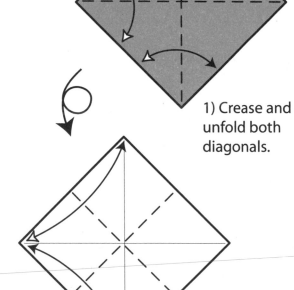

2) Fold corner to corner, crease and unfold in both directions.

3) Collapse the paper down into a smaller square.

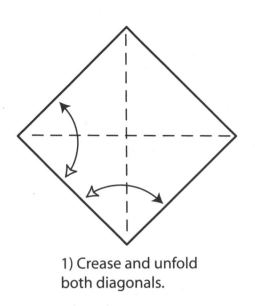

1) Crease and unfold both diagonals.

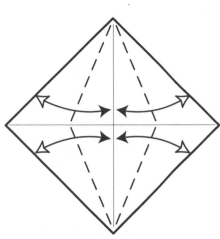

2) Fold each edge to the diagonal, crease and unfold.

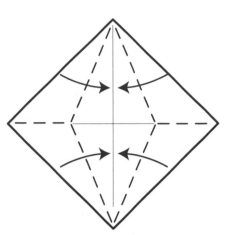

3) Fold each edge towards the diagonal.

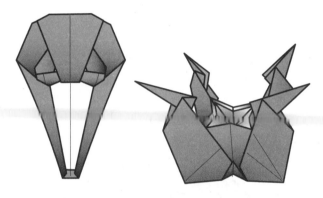

These two models from the book both use the fish base. It's a very flexible base for creating models.

4) Flatten the central flaps downwards.

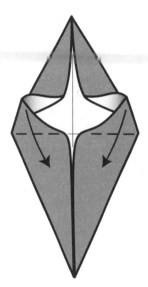

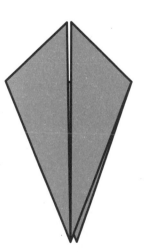

The fish base

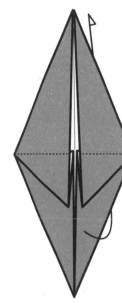

5) Fold the lower half up and behind. Rotate the model.

Cat

Traditional Design

A traditional design is one where the creator is unknown. It usually means the fold has been around for some time.

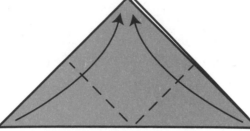

1) Fold in half upwards.

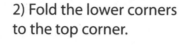

2) Fold the lower corners to the top corner.

You can alter the angle at step 3 to produce different shaped ears.

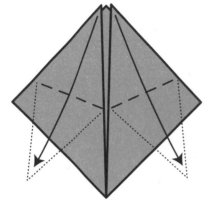

3) Fold the corners down to match the dotted lines.

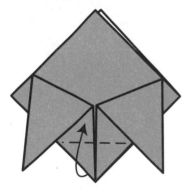

4) Fold the lower corner up between the ears. Turn the paper over.

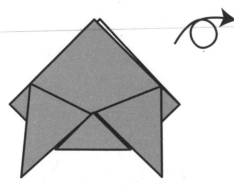

5) This is the result. Turn the model over.

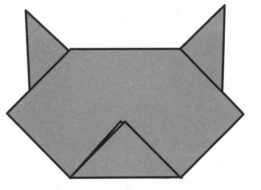

6) Fold up both layers. You can fold the first layer *inside* to achieve a white nose.

Slip-in Fangs

Design by Eric Kenneway

This quick and easy model is great for scaring people!

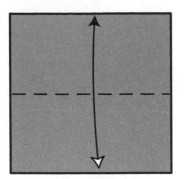

1) Crease in half horizontally.

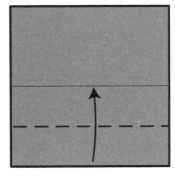

2) Fold the lower edge to the center.

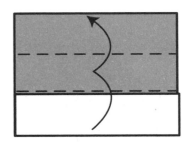

3) Fold over and over.

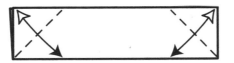

4) Fold and unfold the corners.

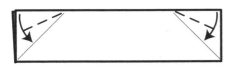

5) Fold the edges to the creases.

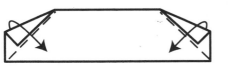

6) Fold over again.

7) Fold over along the folded edges.

The final image is the author at midnight...

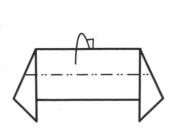

8) Fold the top half behind, creasing firmly.

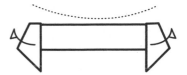

9) Curve slightly, then tuck under your top lip!

Bat

Design by Nick Robinson

This is an example of "Pureland" origami, since it only uses valley and mountain folds. With no complex folds, you can concentrate on neatness.

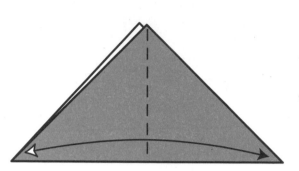

1) Fold in half from corner to opposite corner.

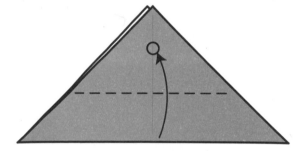

2) Fold from side to side, crease and unfold.

3) Fold the lower edge to the circled point.

When a location isn't clear, a circle can be used to show where the paper should fold to. In the next step, a dotted line performs a similar task.

4) Turn the model over. Fold the top layer down to the dotted line.

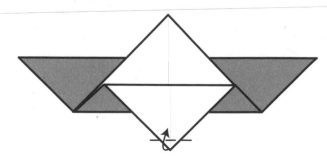

5) Fold the lower corner of the triangle upwards.

12

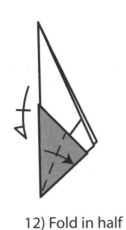

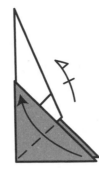

12) Fold in half again, repeat behind.

11) Fold the triangle in half, repeat behind.

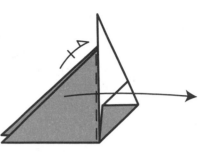

10) Fold a flap over on both sides.

13) Open, rotate and arrange the wings.

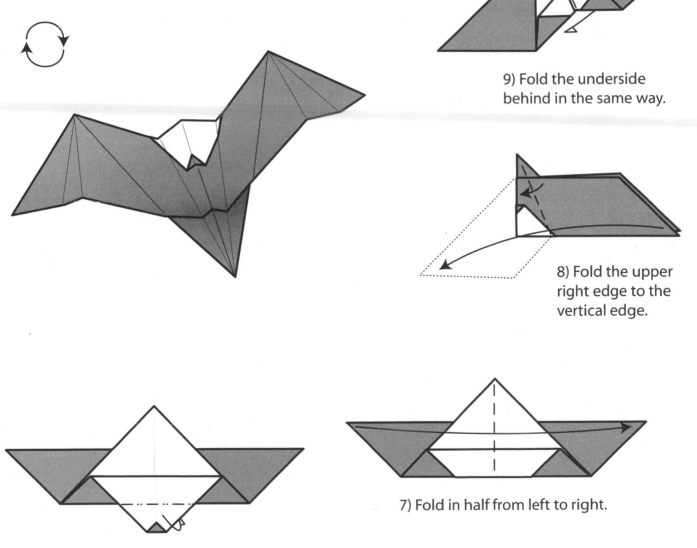

9) Fold the underside behind in the same way.

8) Fold the upper right edge to the vertical edge.

7) Fold in half from left to right.

6) Fold the lower white area underneath.

Goblin

Design by Nick Robinson

This is a simple design, so perfectly suited for folding at short-notice. Try to make the eyes rounded and three-dimensional.

1) Crease a diagonal and unfold.

2) Fold lower edges to the center.

3) Fold upper edges to the center, crease and unfold.

This type of design uses the natural geometry of the paper. Folds are put in very logical places. These types of designs are usually a joy to fold.

4) Push in the corner using an inside reverse fold.

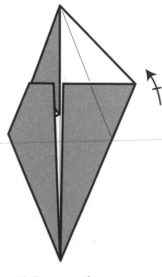

5) Repeat the last step on the other side.

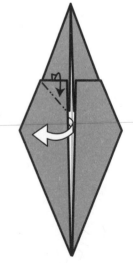

6) Fold the corner over a hidden layer then unfold. Open the left side slightly.

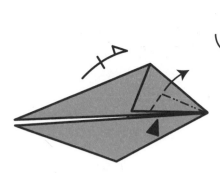

13) Rotate the paper. Squash open the flap to form an eye, repeating behind.

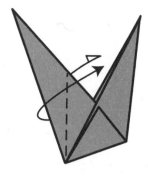

12) Wrap the lower flap around using an outside reverse fold.

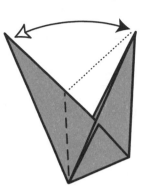

11) Fold so the corners meet, crease and unfold.

The goblin can be made to talk by holding the back of the head in two hands and flexing the paper.

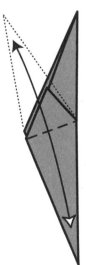

10) Reverse the lower point upwards.

9) Fold the lower corner to the dotted line, crease and unfold.

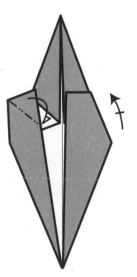

7) Tuck the flap inside the pocket and repeat on the other side.

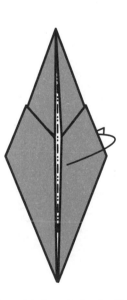

8) Fold the right half of the model behind.

Witch

Design by Nick Robinson

No Halloween book would be complete without a witch or two. Why not try making a life-size head and using it as a mask?

1) Crease a diagonal and unfold.

2) Fold upper edges to the center.

3) The result. Turn the model over.

The profile of a witches hat suggested that the kite base would be a suitable starting point for designing this model.

4) Fold the lower edges to the center, crease and unfold.

5) Fold corner to corner, crease and unfold. Turn over.

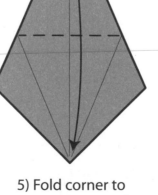

6) Fold the inner corners to match the dotted lines. The next drawing shows the circled area.

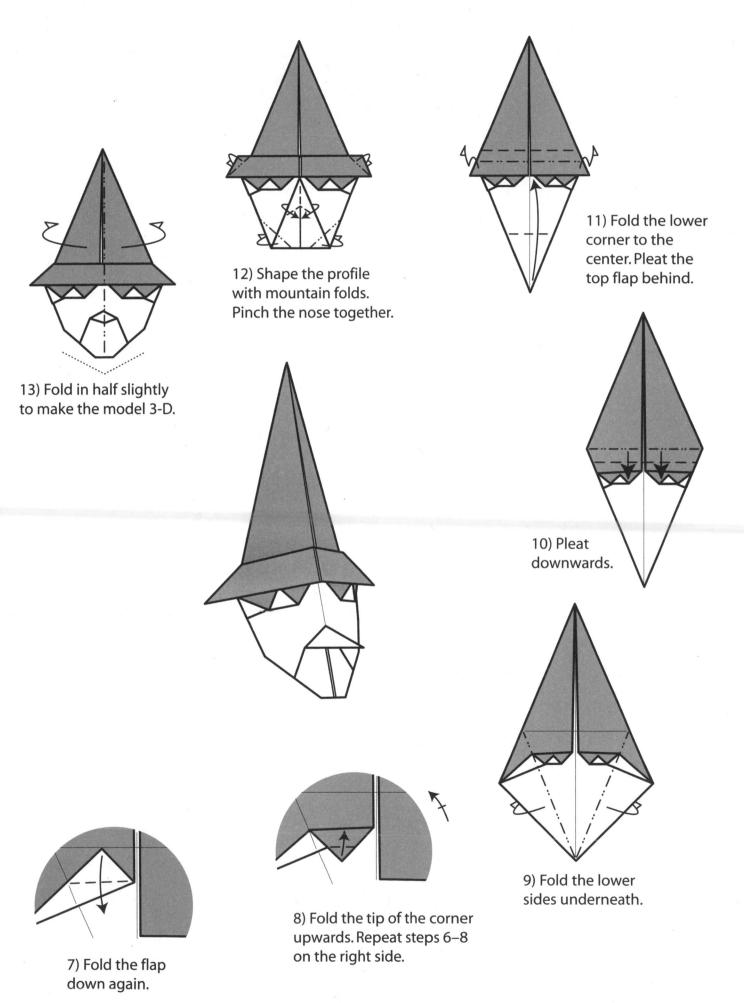

12) Shape the profile with mountain folds. Pinch the nose together.

11) Fold the lower corner to the center. Pleat the top flap behind.

13) Fold in half slightly to make the model 3-D.

10) Pleat downwards.

9) Fold the lower sides underneath.

7) Fold the flap down again.

8) Fold the tip of the corner upwards. Repeat steps 6–8 on the right side.

Pumpkin

Design by Nick Robinson

This classic Halloween model lends itself to many variations by altering the folds in step 9.

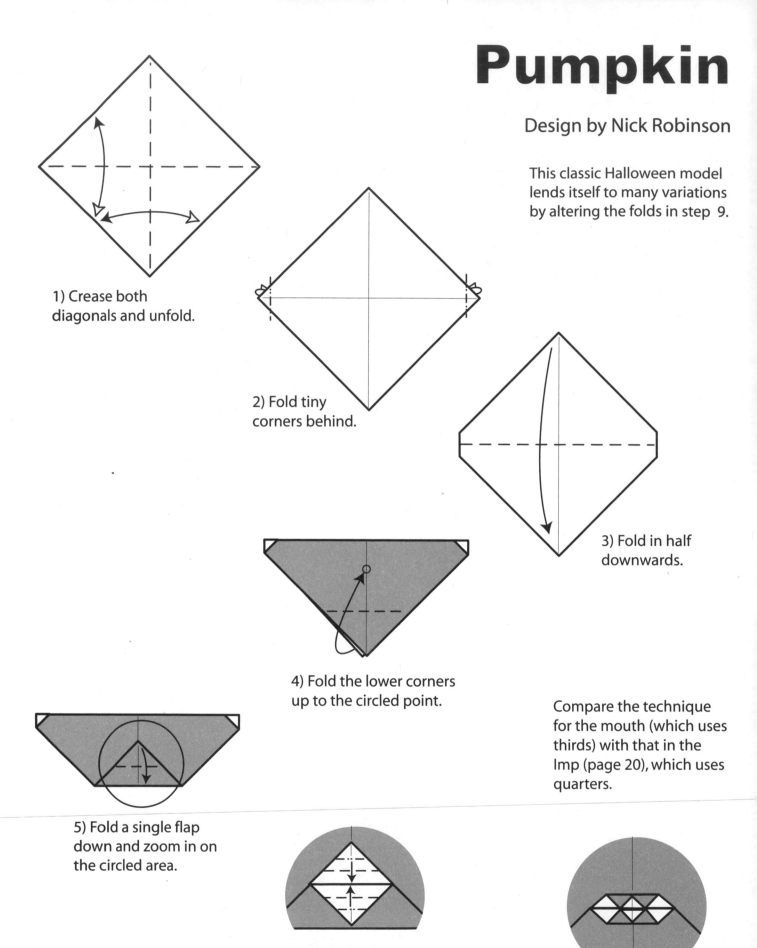

1) Crease both diagonals and unfold.

2) Fold tiny corners behind.

3) Fold in half downwards.

4) Fold the lower corners up to the circled point.

Compare the technique for the mouth (which uses thirds) with that in the Imp (page 20), which uses quarters.

5) Fold a single flap down and zoom in on the circled area.

6) Pleat the paper into thirds (just guess!)

7) The finished pleating.

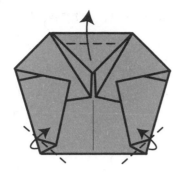

 13) Fold the top corner up, leaving a gap. Round the lower corners. Turn the model over.

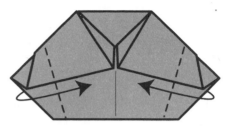 12) Fold the sides inwards.

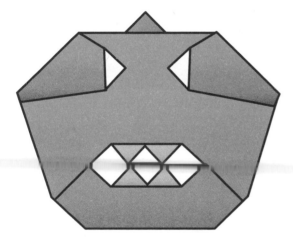

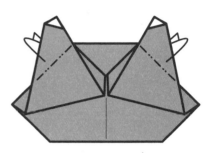 11) Wrap the top flaps behind, creasing firmly.

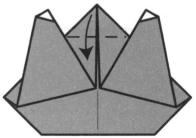 10) Fold the top corner down.

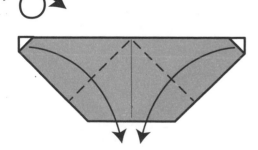 8) Turn the model over. Fold the upper edges to lie on the vertical center.

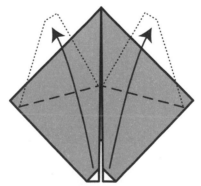 9) Fold both lower corners to match the dotted lines.

Imp

Design by Nick Robinson

This is an "action" model, because the mouth can be made to open and close by flexing the creases in step 14.

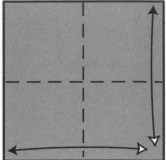

1) Fold in half from side to side and unfold in both directions.

2) Turn over, rotate and crease a vertical diagonal.

3) Fold side corners to the center.

4) Fold in half upwards.

This model uses a well-established technique (steps 9–12) for creating teeth. You'll find this on many origami models, including others in this book. The paper is divided into 4, but you can create more teeth by dividing into 6 or 8 pleats.

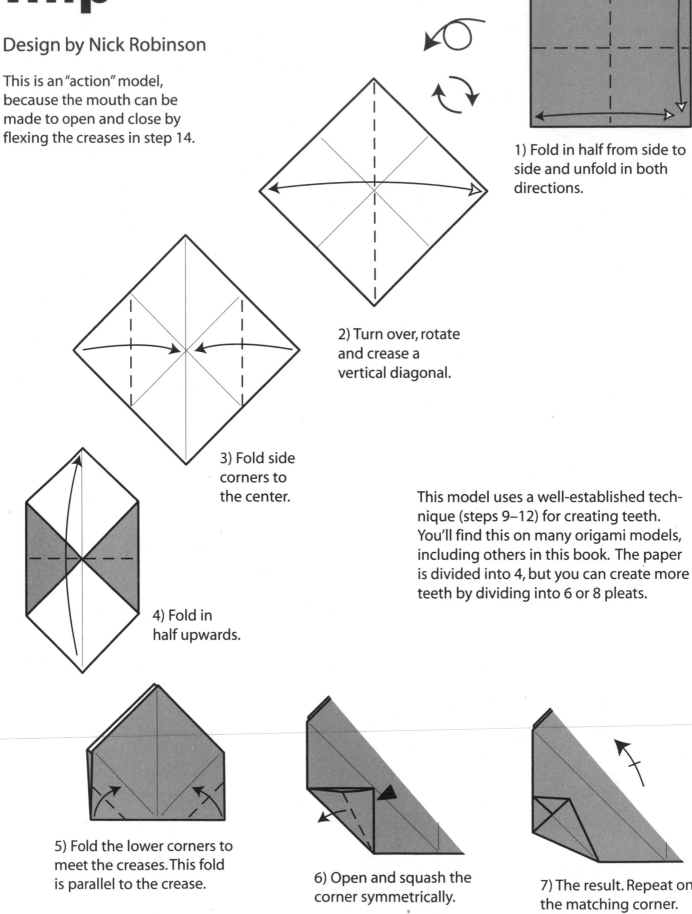

5) Fold the lower corners to meet the creases. This fold is parallel to the crease.

6) Open and squash the corner symmetrically.

7) The result. Repeat on the matching corner.

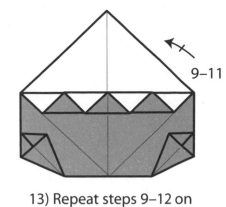

13) Repeat steps 9–12 on the upper triangle.

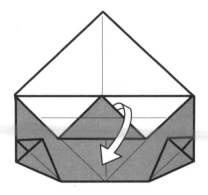

12) Pleat using these creases.

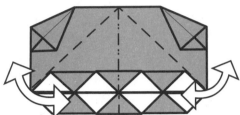

14) Rotate the paper. Hold by the eyes and squeeze inwards to open the mouth.

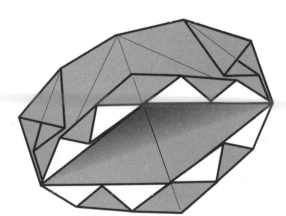

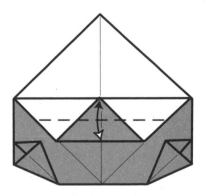

11) Unfold the triangle.

10) Fold the triangle in half and unfold.

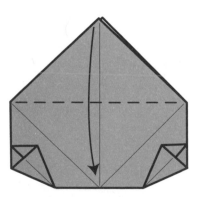

8) Fold a single corner down to the bottom center.

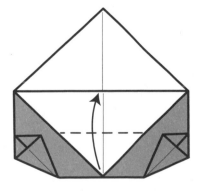

9) Fold the same corner to the center.

Ghost

Design by Nick Robinson

Ghosts have a very vague
shape, so we can fold them in
many different ways. White
paper is generally best!

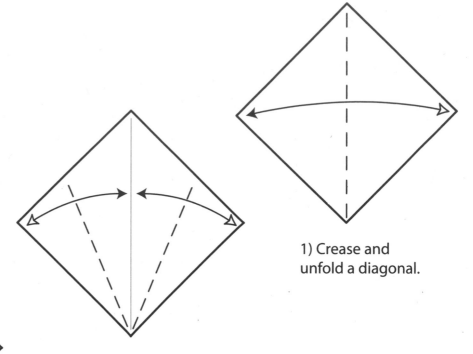

1) Crease and
unfold a diagonal.

2) Fold both lower edges to
the center, crease and unfold.

3) Fold in half downwards.

4) Fold the first
layer up so the
circled points meet.

The final shaping and rounding is
what gives life to this model. If you
fold from thicker paper and
dampen it slightly, it will hold a
curved shape when dry. This
technique is called "wet folding."

5) Fold back
down, then turn
the paper over.

6) Fold each upper corner to
the bottom corner. Turn over.

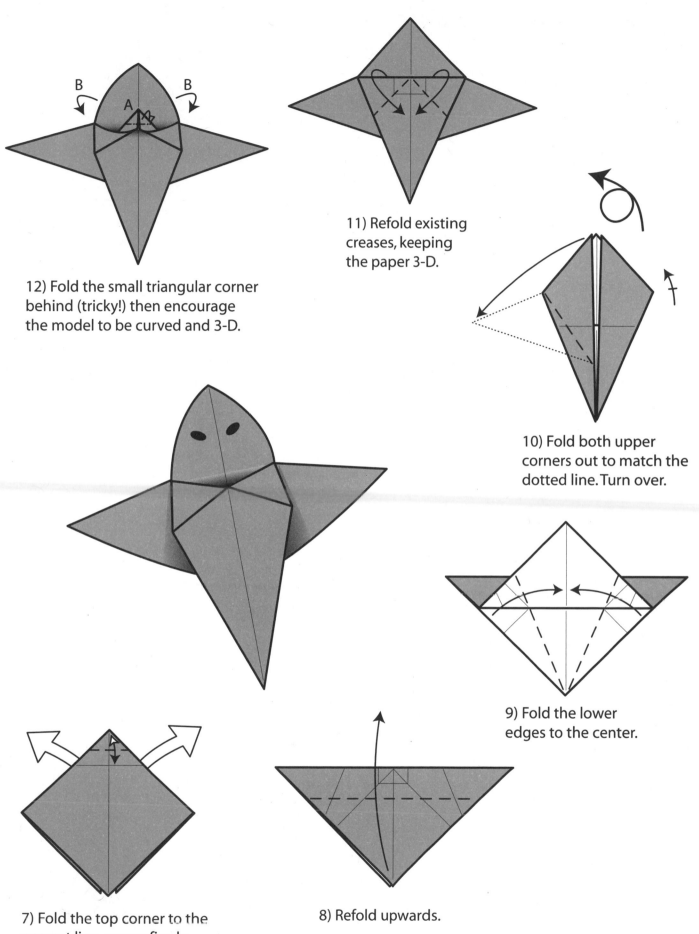

B   B
A

12) Fold the small triangular corner behind (tricky!) then encourage the model to be curved and 3-D.

11) Refold existing creases, keeping the paper 3-D.

10) Fold both upper corners out to match the dotted line. Turn over.

9) Fold the lower edges to the center.

7) Fold the top corner to the nearest line, crease firmly, then unfold the rear flaps.

8) Refold upwards.

Flying Witch

Design by Nick Robinson

This design uses two squares of paper, one for the witch and another for the broom. Try to find and use suitable colors for each.

1) Crease a diagonal and unfold.

2) Fold upper edges to the center.

3) The result. Turn the model over.

Given the range of techniques available, it would be possible to create this figure from a single square. However it would demand more skill and be less simple to fold.

4) Fold the top corner to the bottom corner.

5) Leave a small gap, then fold the flap back upwards.

6) Fold the left half underneath.

12) Reverse the point back inside.

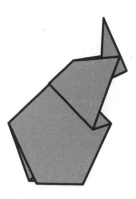

13) The witch is complete. Continue to make the broomstick.

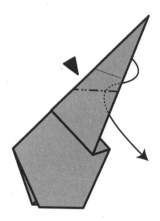

11) Reverse fold the top point inside.

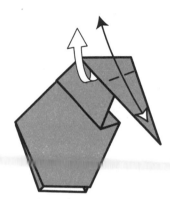

10) Fold the corner again to match the dotted line, then unfold to step 9.

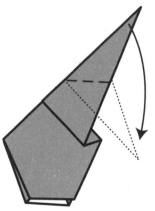

9) Fold the corner down to match the dotted line.

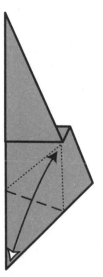

7) Fold the corner to match the dotted line, then unfold.

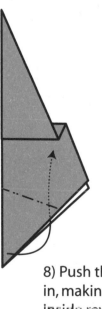

8) Push the corner in, making an inside reverse fold.

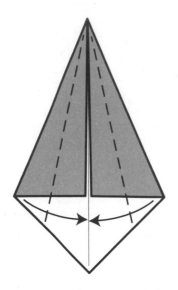

14) Start with step 3 of the Witch. Fold the long edges to the center.

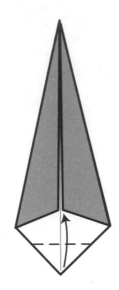

15) Fold the corner upwards.

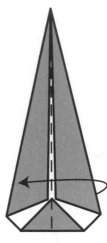

16) Fold in half.

17) Fold a flap over to the dotted line.

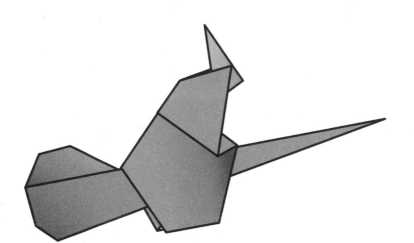

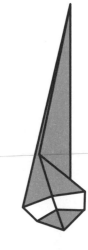

18) Turn the model over.

19) Wrap the Witch around the broomstick, using glue to attach if your principles allow it!

Vampire Mail

Francis Ow, adapted by Michel Grand

Some origami models are practical as well as decorative. This envelope will certainly give the mailman a fright!

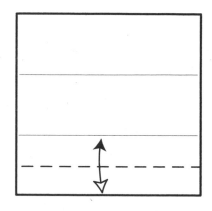

1) Start creased into thirds. Fold the lower edge to the nearest crease and unfold.

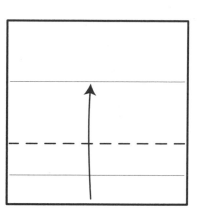

2) Fold upwards.

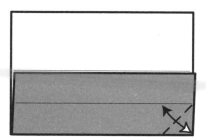

3) Fold the corner to the crease, then unfold.

There is a small but dedicated group who love to design and post origami envelopes. They are known as ELFA—the Envelope and Letter Folding Association.

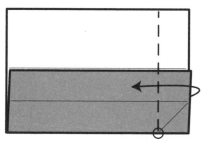

4) Fold the left edge over, starting at the circled point.

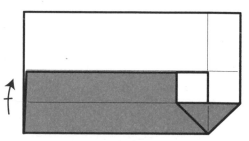

5) Open the layer again, squashing the bottom corner.

6) Repeat the last three steps on the left side.

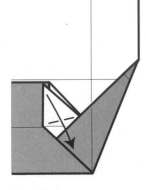

12) Fold the corner down at a slight angle.

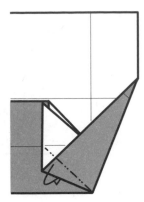

11) Fold the flap underneath.

The move here is known as a "swivel fold." It is a very flexible technique.

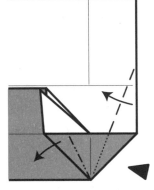

10) Adjust the colored triangle so it changes into a larger triangle.

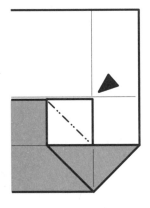

9) Inside reverse the corner.

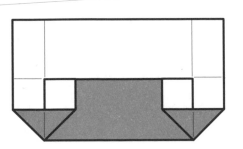

7) The paper should look like this.

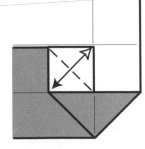

8) Fold the white square in half, then unfold.

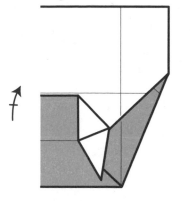

13) Repeat the last five steps on the left.

This design is an adaptation of an original model. See if you can adjust the proportions and create yet another variation!

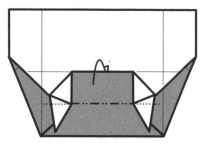

14) Fold the flap behind.

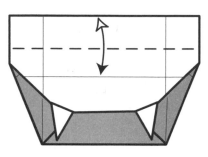

15) Fold the top edge to the horizontal crease, then unfold.

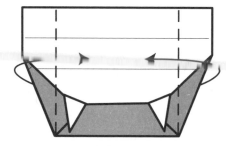

16) Fold the sides inwards.

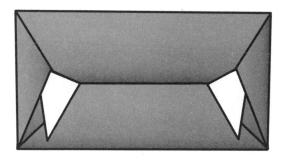

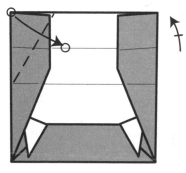

17) Fold the upper corner to the horizontal crease. Repeat on the right.

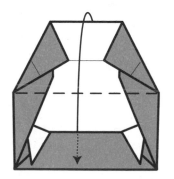

18) Fold the top edge down and tuck it into the pocket.

Cat's Head

Design by David Petty

This is an example of how altering a base can produce a model that looks quite unusual.

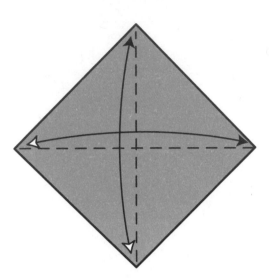

1) Fold in half from corner to opposite corner then unfold, in both directions.

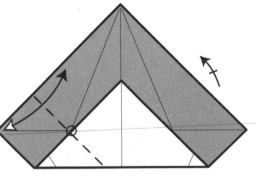

2) Fold the upper sides to the center, crease and unfold.

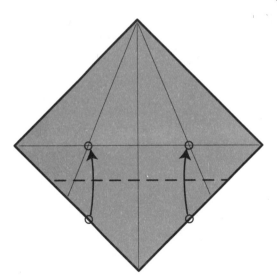

3) Fold the lower corner upwards so that the circled lines meet.

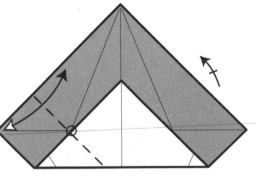

4) Fold the left corner at right angles to the edge, the crease passes through the circled intersection. Unfold and repeat.

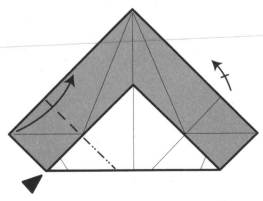

5) Reverse the white corner inside. Repeat on the right.

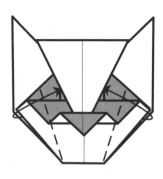

11) Fold the side flaps in, tucking under the central flap.

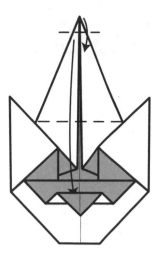

10) Fold the tip of the top corner over, then fold the upper flap down under the nose.

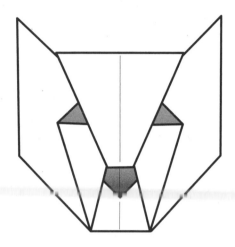

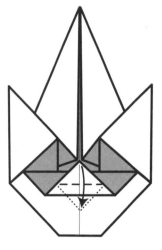

9) Fold the same corner down again.

This is an "offset preliminary base," combined with half a fish base.

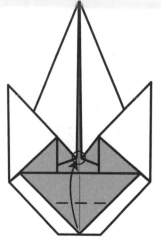

8) Fold the lower colored corner to the circled area.

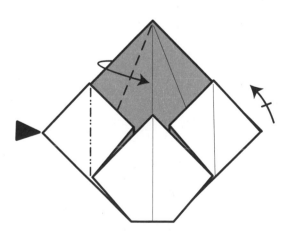

6) Reverse the white corner inside while folding the colored edge to the vertical center. Repeat on the right.

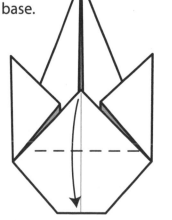

7) Fold the inner corner to touch the lower edge.

Fright Mask

Design by Wayne Brown & Nick Robinson

This model is of the scary mask that people love to wear during Halloween. It was created as a collaboration between two folding friends.

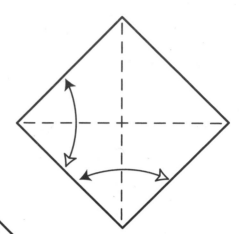

1) Crease both diagonals and unfold.

2) Fold lower edges to the center, crease only where shown and unfold.

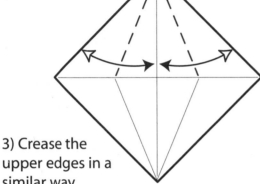

3) Crease the upper edges in a similar way.

Narrow angle folds (such as in step 4) require a little more concentration to make them accurate.

4) Fold lower edges to the nearest crease, then unfold.

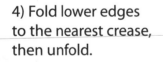

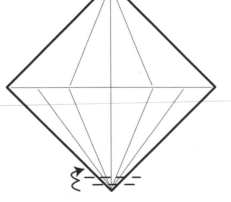

5) Fold the bottom corner over and over a little way.

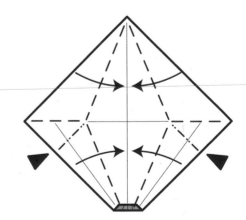

6) Fold the sides in together. The mountain folds are formed as you flatten the flaps downwards.

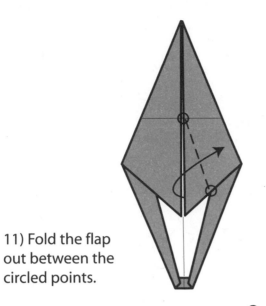

11) Fold the flap out between the circled points.

12) Open and squash the corner (refer to the next drawing).

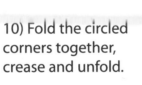

10) Fold the circled corners together, crease and unfold.

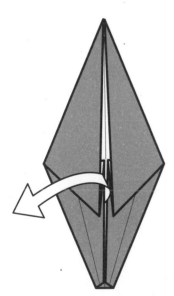

7) Open the left side out slightly.

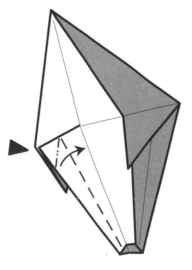

8) Refold on the existing valley crease, squashing the top corner symmetrically.

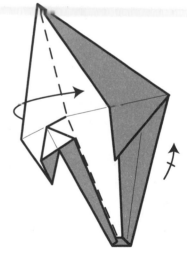

9) Fold the model flat again and repeat steps 7–9 on the other side.

33

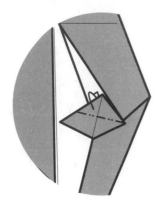

13) Fold the corner inside.

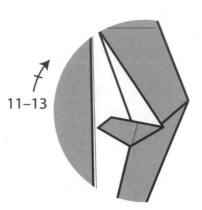

11–13

14) Repeat steps 11–13 on the left side.

This model was inspired by Quentin Trollip's "Scream," which achieves a similar result through a different method.

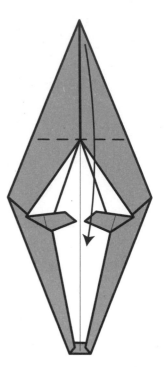

15) Fold down on an existing crease.

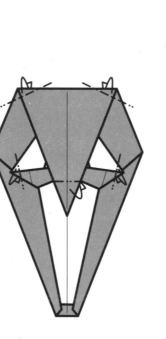

16) Tuck the point of the flap underneath. Shape the eyes and the top edge with small mountain folds.

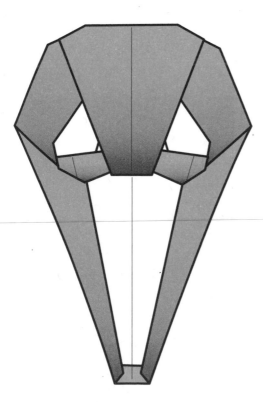

If you use slightly thicker paper, you can add gentle curves to the edges, to make it more flowing and less geometric.

Fangs

Design by Eric Kenneway

There have been several different versions of this model created over the years. For some reason it seems to fascinate creators.

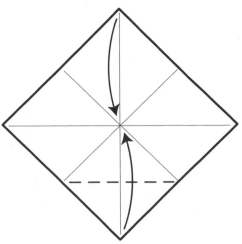

1) Fold and unfold a preliminary base. (page 8) Fold opposite corners to the center.

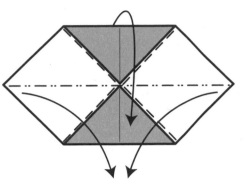

2) Refold the preliminary base.

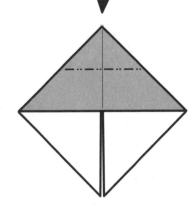

3) Fold the top to the center, crease firmly and unfold.

4) Sink the corner.

"Sinking" can be a nightmare for new folders, but try to understand the principle of what is happening. Most of the creases in the sunken area are simply the reverse of what they were.

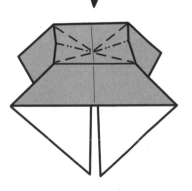

5) The step in progress.

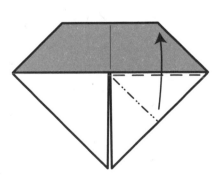

6) Fold the flap up, then down in half.

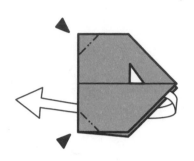

13) Push in the corners, open 3/4 of the way and rotate.

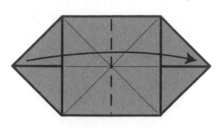

12) Fold in half from left to right.

Step 13—You will often see small inside reverse folds shown this way. You can precrease the folds by making a valley first, or just "go for it."

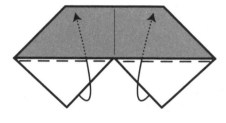

11) Fold down and flatten the top layer.

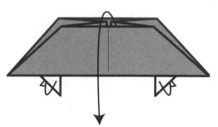

10) Fold the corners up, tucking them into pockets.

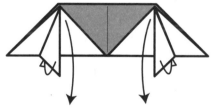

9) Fold the white flaps down, including the lowest flaps.

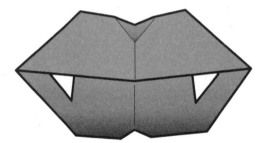

6–7

8) Repeat steps 6 and 7 on the left.

7) Fold the corner down to match the dotted line.

Trick or Treat?

Design by Gilad Aharoni

For many years it has been traditional to give small candies to people who call. This little treat has a trick up its sleeve—it bites!

1) Start with both diagonals creased. Fold upper and lower corners to the center and turn over.

2) Fold upper and lower edges to the center, allowing hidden corners to "flip" out from behind.

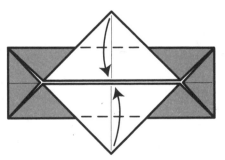

3) Fold left and right corners inwards.

4) Fold upper and lower corners to the center.

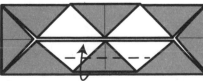

5) Fold the first edge at the bottom to the center.

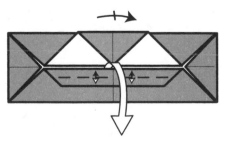

6) Fold the narrow flap in half, then open out the corner. Repeat the last two steps on the upper half.

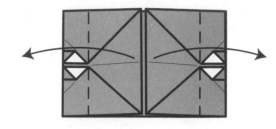

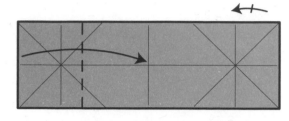

11) Fold the left edge to the center. Repeat on the right.

12) The picture is enlarged. Fold the flaps back out again on both sides.

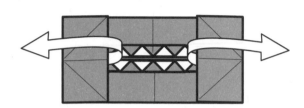

10) Unfold the flaps and turn the paper over.

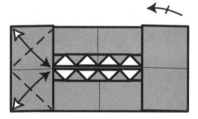

9) Fold the corners to the horizontal crease, then unfold. Repeat on the right.

In order to create neat teeth at step 8, the creasing during steps 4–6 needs to be sharp and accurate.

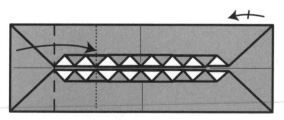

8) Fold the short side to the dotted line. Repeat on the right.

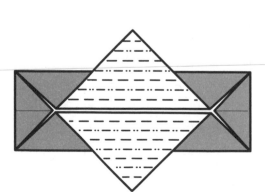

7) Pleat the white triangles towards the center.

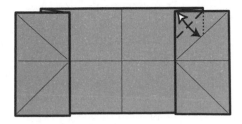

12) Fold corner to the hidden edge, crease and unfold.

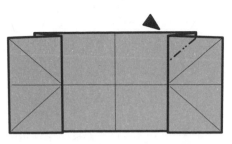

12) Inside reverse the corner.

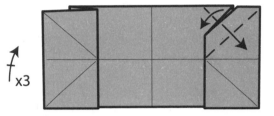

13) Fold the edge over, opening and rotating it—check the next picture. Repeat the last three steps on each corner.

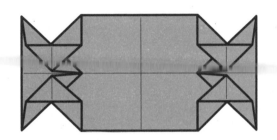

14) The model looks like this. Turn the paper over.

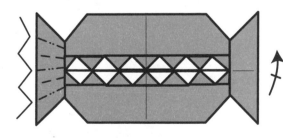

15) Make rough pleats, repeating on the right.

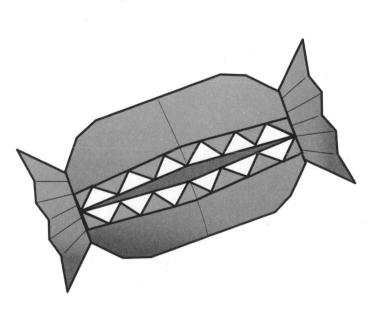

Finger Trap

Design by Ilan Garibaldi

This wonderful trick uses the tension in the paper to snap shut. It works best from slightly thicker, crisper paper.

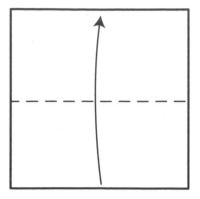

1) Fold in half upwards.

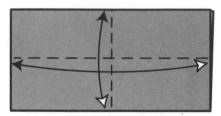

2) Fold in half then unfold, both ways.

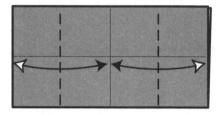

3) Fold the short edges to the center, crease and unfold.

Step 6 *looks* tricky, but just emphasize the creases shown and it will flatten easily.

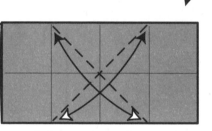

4) Crease two diagonals in the central square.

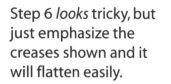
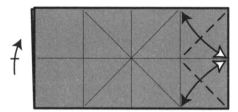

5) Crease diagonals in the outer corners. Repeat on the left and turn the paper over.

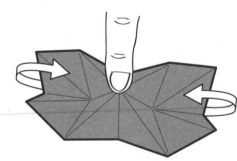

8) Press in the center, the trap will close!

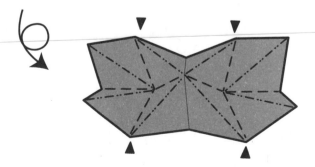

6) Collapse the paper into 2-D using these (existing) creases.

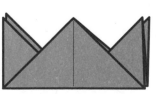

7) Flatten the paper firmly. Carefully open the model to the previous step.

Claws

Design by Nick Robinson

This is a simple concept for a model and several creators have made one. Make a test fold to see what size paper works best, then make a claw for every finger, using dark colored paper.

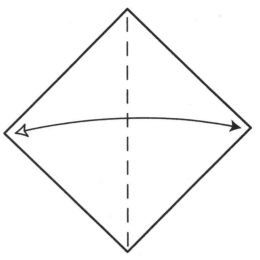

1) Fold in half from side to side, then unfold.

2) Fold the lower sides to the center.

3) Fold the white triangle down.

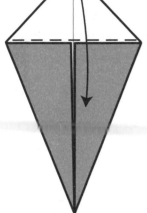

The Kite Base seen in step 3 is a great starting point for designing your own simple models.

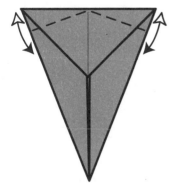

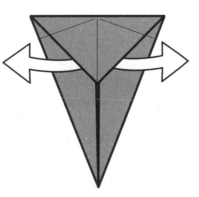

4) Fold the upper corners back down the outer edges, crease and unfold.

5) Unfold the lower flaps.

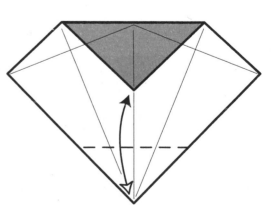

6) Fold the lower corner to the inner corner, crease and unfold.

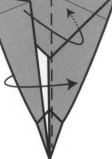

13) Fold in half, tucking the corner on the left into the pocket on the right.

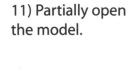

12) Ease out the lower flap, tucking the upper corner underneath it.

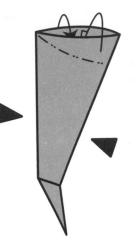

11) Partially open the model.

The folds in steps 10 and 13 are used to "lock" the paper together. These moves are often very ingenious!

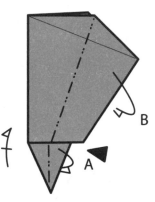

14) Open and tuck the upper edge inside. Round the model.

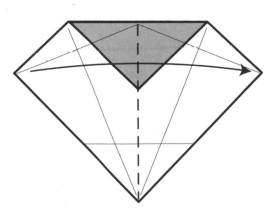

10) Wrap the sides inside, making a small squash to flatten the paper. Repeat underneath.

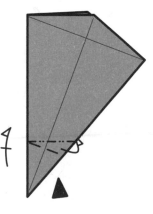

9) Make a crimp, folding the paper inside. Repeat underneath.

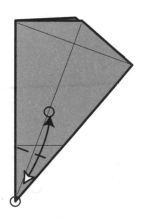

8) Fold the corner back along the center crease starting at the horizontal crease. Unfold.

7) Fold in half from left to right.

Gargoyle

Design by Nick Robinson

This is a perfect subject for origami, since every gargoyle you see on a church will be totally different. It is said that the stone masons modeled them of their enemies!

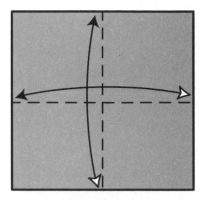

1) Fold in half side to side, crease and unfold. Repeat in the other direction.

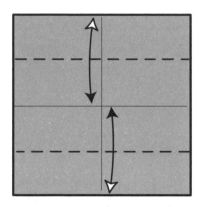

2) Fold upper and lower edges to the center, crease and unfold. Turn over.

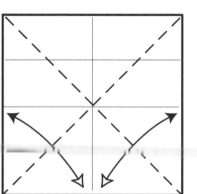

3) Crease and unfold both diagonals.

Try to find some paper with a texture to it, so that the finished model will look as if it has actually been made from stone.

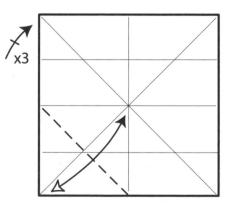

4) Fold each corner to the center, crease and unfold.

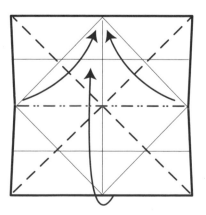

5) Collapse the paper upwards using the creases shown.

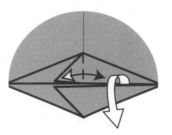

11) Unfold the lower half. Crease and unfold the central upper flap.

12) Squash the triangular flap symmetrically.

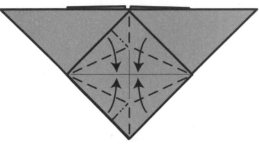

10) Make two rabbit ear folds.

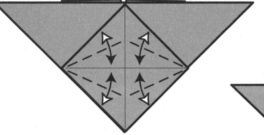

9) Fold each edge of the square to the horizontal center line, crease firmly and unfold.

8) Fold the first flap in half upwards.

Dotted lines are a good way to show folds that take place on hidden layers.

7) This is the result. Turn the model over.

6) Fold the center of the top edge down, flattening on the hidden (dotted) creases.

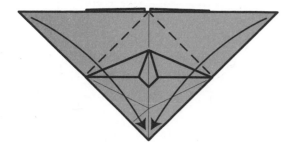

13) Fold the upper corners to the lower corner.

14) Open and squash both points.

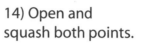
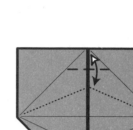

15) Fold the top to the hidden corner, creasing firmly through all layers, between the creases.

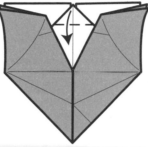

16) Open layers and fold over a small triangular flap. Close the layers.

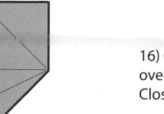
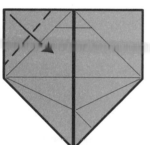

17) Fold the corner in at a slight angle.

Experiment with the fold made at step 17. You can produce many different shaped ears this way.

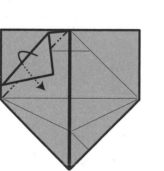

18) Fold the flap back into a pocket on an existing crease.

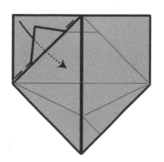

19) Tuck the triangular flap into the same pocket.

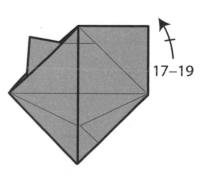

17–19

20) Repeat steps 17–19 on the other side.

If you struggle here, go and have cup of tea, then try again.

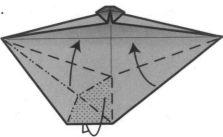

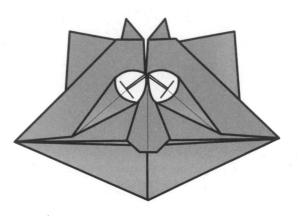

26) Fold the dotted area underneath as you refold the flap as in step 10.

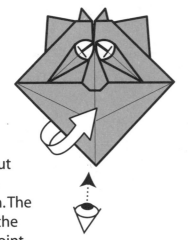

25) Open out paper from underneath. The eye shows the next viewpoint.

The 3-D folding in step 23 takes a little practice, but it adds a lot of life to the eye.

24) Shape the nose and the horns.

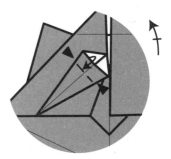

23) Fold the colored edge over, opening and rounding the eye. Repeat steps 21–23 on the other eye.

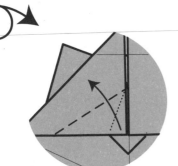

22) Squash open the flap.

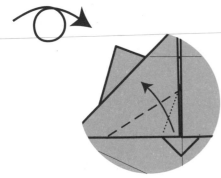

21) Fold a corner over.

Grasping Hand

Design by Nick Robinson

This model uses a technique to create fingers that was first used by Jun Maekawa as part of his classic "demon" design.

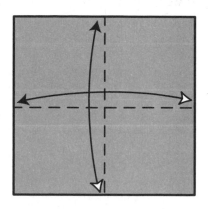

1) Fold in half side to opposite side, crease and unfold. Repeat in the other direction.

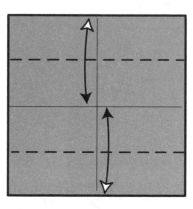

2) Fold upper and lower edges to the center, crease and unfold. Turn over.

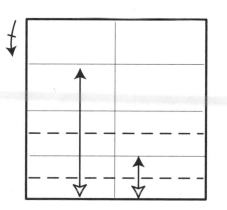

3) Add 1/8th and 3/8th creases, repeating on the upper half.

Models like this that have a lot of initial ("pre") creasing require you to fold carefully and accurately. This ability has to be worked on and usually means folding slightly more slowly than usual. Make sure the overhead lighting is bright.

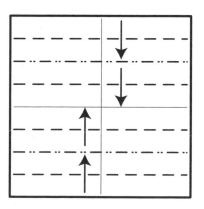

4) Pleat the sides inwards.

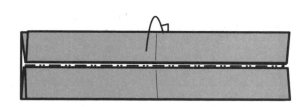

5) Fold the upper half behind.

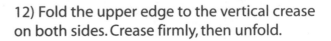

12) Fold the upper edge to the vertical crease on both sides. Crease firmly, then unfold.

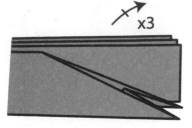

11) Repeat steps 6–10 on the remaining three corners.

Whilst it is possible to make the folds in steps 6–10 through more than one flap, the resulting creases won't be as sharp as if you make them individually.

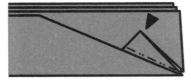

10) Inside reverse the white corner.

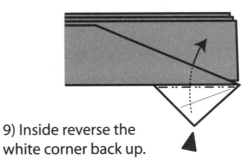

9) Inside reverse the white corner back up.

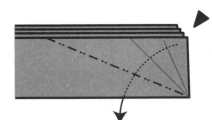

8) Reverse the corner inside.

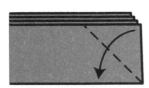

6) Fold a single corner over.

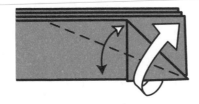

7) Fold the angled edge to the bottom, creasing firmly through both layers.

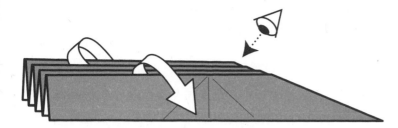

13) Open the layers apart—
check the next drawing.

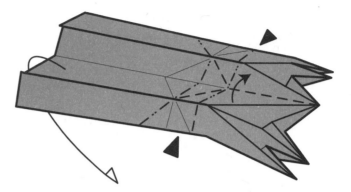

13) Fold the rear end downwards
using the mountain crease.
Collapse the front end together.

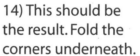

14) This should be
the result. Fold the
corners underneath.

When you have
finished the model,
fold something small
and tempting to put
under the hand.

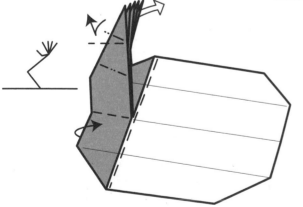

15) Form a thumb, then shape
the arm to match the profile
shown. Finally, angle the colored
section forward slightly.

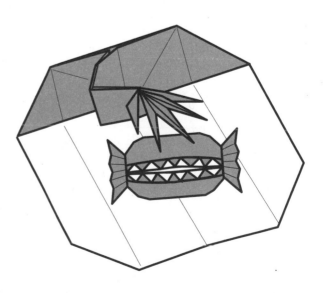

Witches Brew

Design by Simon Phillips and Tony Ayres

These two designers published a small book of original origami in 1974 and have never been heard from since! This design is well worth sharing, even nearly 40 years later!

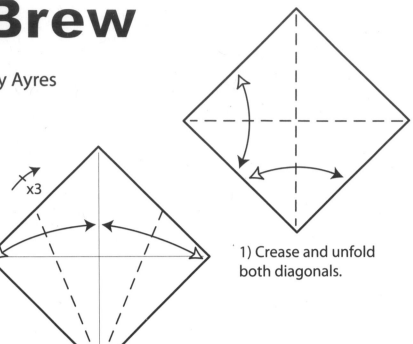

1) Crease and unfold both diagonals.

2) Fold the lower edges to the center, crease and unfold. Repeat from each corner.

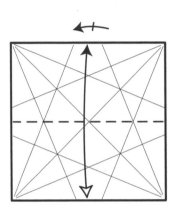

3) Rotate the paper. Fold in half, crease and unfold, in both directions.

When you fold and unfold to add creases that will be used later, it is known as "precreasing".

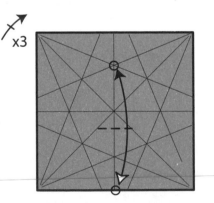

4) Turn the paper over. Fold so the circled points meet, creasing only where shown. Repeat three more times.

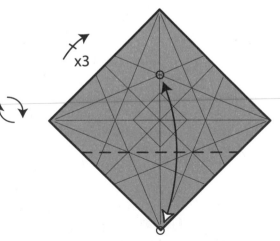

5) Rotate slightly and fold so the circled points meet. Repeat three more times.

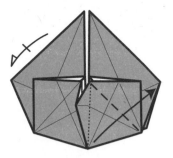

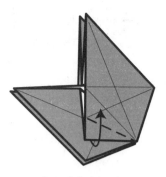

11) Lift the central point on both sides, as shown here. Make the valley fold, with a hidden mountain fold. Make the same folds on the other side.

12) Fold the short edge to the crease.

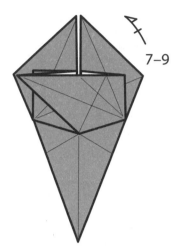

10) Repeat steps 7–9 on the underside.

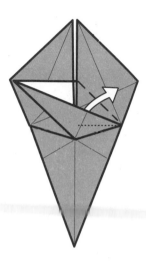

9) Carefully pull out paper to match the other side.

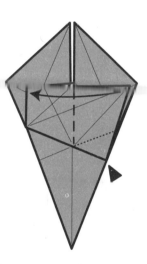

8) Fold the flap to the left, flattening on the hidden crease.

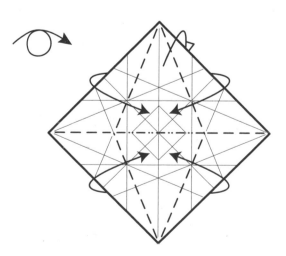

6) Turn the paper over and fold into a fish base (see page 9).

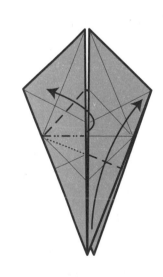

7) Open the left side slightly and make the folds shown. Dont add any new creases!

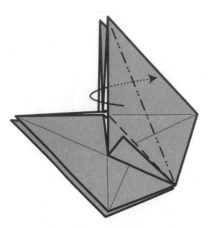

13) Tuck paper into the pocket, easing a layer out from the small triangular flap.

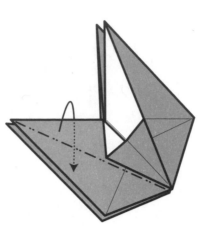

14) Fold a flap inside on the right so things are symmetrical.

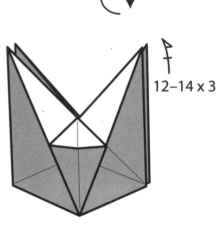

12–14 x 3

15) Rotate slightly. Repeat steps 12–14 underneath and between the left and right layers.

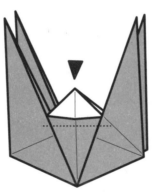

16) Open slightly and sink the top corner on existing creases.

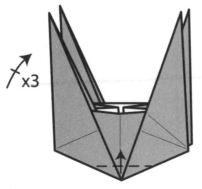

x3

17) Fold the lower corner up a little way. Repeat on three matching corners.

18) Fold the point down so it touches the horizontal edge.

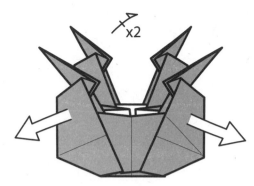

23) Gently ease each witch backwards so the cauldron opens slightly.

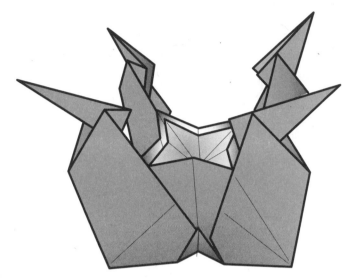

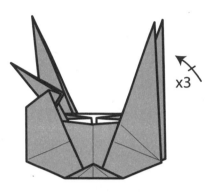

22) Repeat steps 18–21 on the three other flaps.

When making the witches, don't fold them identically, but give each one some character.

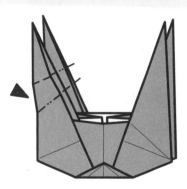

21) Reverse the point in and back out again.

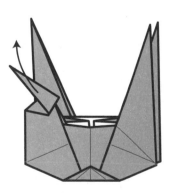

20) Unfold the last two steps.

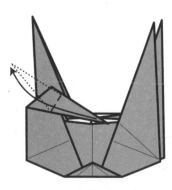

19) Fold it back to the dotted line.

Cauldron

Traditional, adapted by Nick Robinson

This is based on a traditional design, sometimes known as "Verdi's Vase." It's thought to be Chinese in origin.

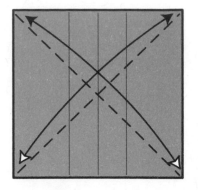

1) Start creased in half and into thirds. Crease and unfold both diagonals.

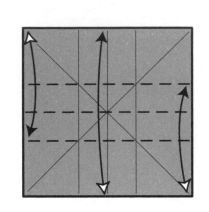

2) Add matching horizontal creases.

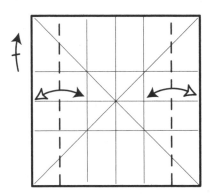

3) Add outer 1/6th creases repeating horizontally.

It is essential to make accurate, sharp creases throughout, or the later stages may be more difficult. Fold slowly and crease only when you are in *exactly* the right place.

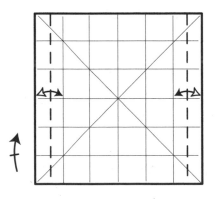

4) Add outer 1/12th creases repeating horizontally

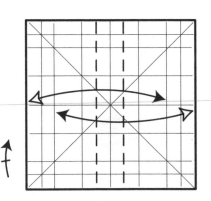

5) Add inner 1/12th creases repeating horizontally.

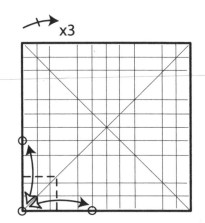

6) Add two small creases, repeating on each corner.

This should be easier than it looks, since the creases are already in the right direction.

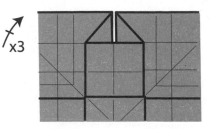

13) The move complete. Repeat on the other three corners.

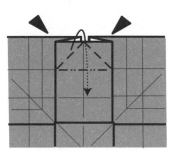

12) Fold the triangular flap inside.

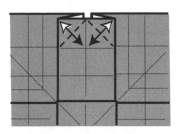

11) Fold the corners to the nearest horizontal crease. Crease and unfold.

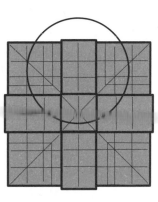

10) We'll zoom in on the circled area.

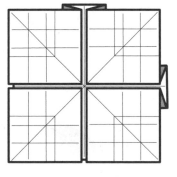

9) This is the result. Turn the paper over.

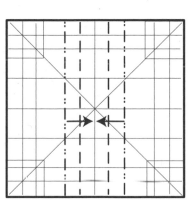

7) Pleat together at the center.

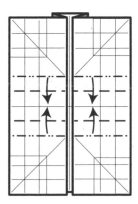

8) Pleat in the opposite direction.

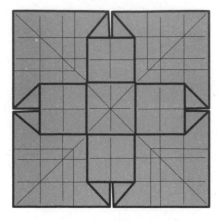

14) The paper should look like this. Turn the model over.

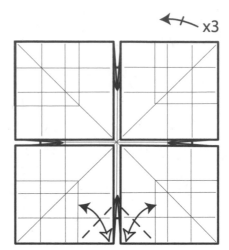

15) Fold the corners to the nearest vertical creases, then unfold. Repeat three times.

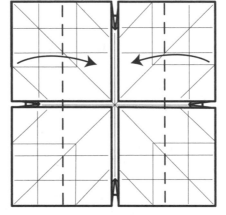

16) Fold left and right sides to the center.

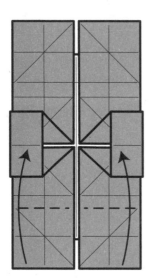

17) Fold the lower side to the center.

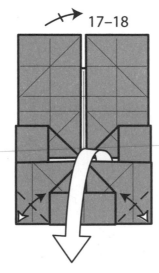

18) Make firm precreases, repeating steps 17 and 18 on the other end. Unfold to step 17.

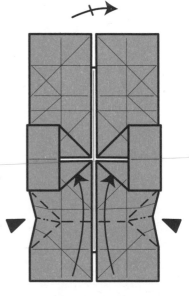

19) Fold the lower side under the layers, making a reverse fold as you go. Repeat on the other end.

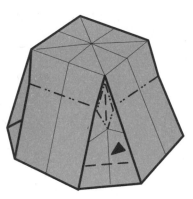

24) The move completed. Repeat on the other three corners.

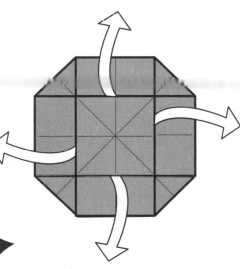

23) Put a finger inside the model, pressing out the creases shown. The lower section curves inwards.

22) Carefully ease out trapped paper.

This move is tricky—you should be very gentle with the paper. Open a little way, then move to the next corner, keep working slowly round.

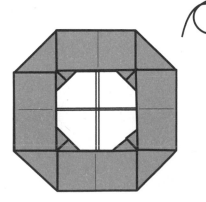

21) This should be the result. Turn the paper over.

20) Fold the flap underneath. Repeat three times.

Horrors

Design by Robert Neale

Despite being over 40 years old, this model is still fresh and exciting. The way the final model is manipulated is highly innovative and clever.

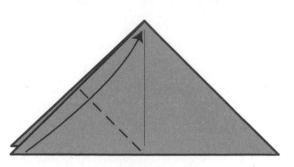

1) Start with a waterbomb base (see page 8). Fold the corner on the left to the top.

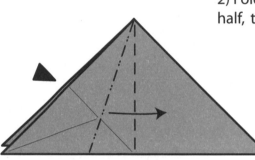

2) Fold the uppermost flap in half, then unfold back to step 1.

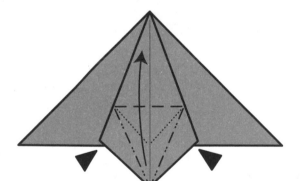

3) Squash the flap using the creases shown.

Step 8 shows a form known as the "Frog Base." There are always different methods to achieve most folds, try to find the most satisfying.

4) Fold the lower corner up, folding the sides inwards.

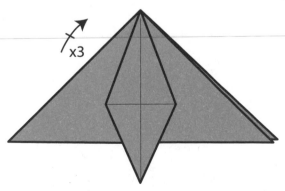

5) Fold the narrow flap down.

6) Repeat steps 1–5 on the other three corners.

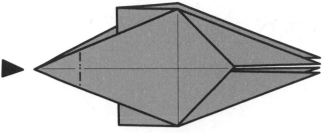

12) Sink the point inside. This will involve partially opening the model and making the indicated mountain crease on all layers. Be patient!

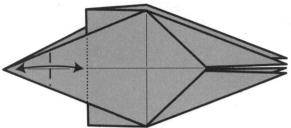

11) Fold the left corner to the hidden (dotted) edge. Make this crease very firmly, then unfold.

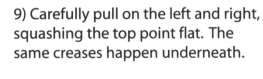

10) This is the view from overhead. Swing the left half underneath.

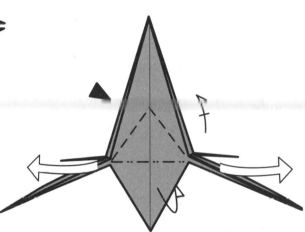

9) Carefully pull on the left and right, squashing the top point flat. The same creases happen underneath.

Getting from step 9 to 10 will require some patience. When you have managed it, unfold the step and analyze how it works.

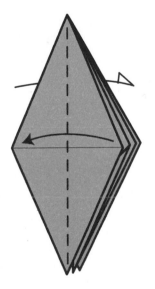

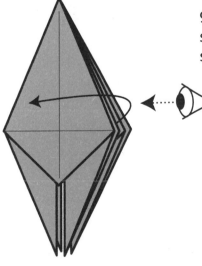

7) Fold the first layer on the right over to the left. Repeat the move underneath.

8) Open two layers and look where indicated.

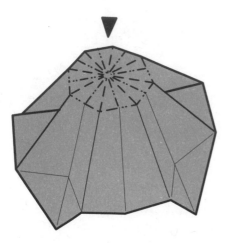

13) The sink in progress, collapse the paper flat.

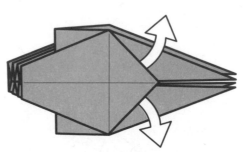

14) Open out hidden layers.

Step 13 is a complex sink. If you can manage this, sinks will no longer be a problem!

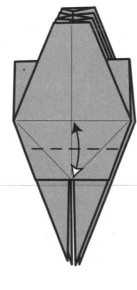

15) Fold and unfold on existing creases to add them to the upper colored layer.

16) Fold the upper corner inside. Repeat on the lower corner. Rotate the model clockwise.

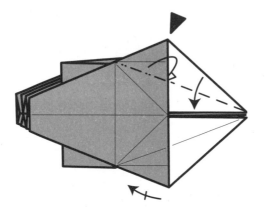

17) Fold the lower horizontal edge to the crease line, then unfold.

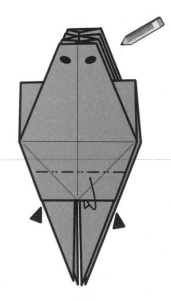

18) Reverse fold the flap inside. Add "ghost eyes."

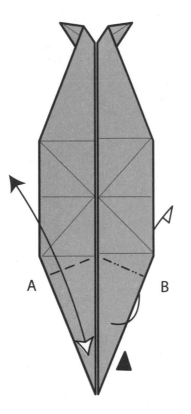

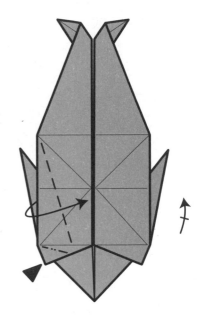

23) Make the long valley crease, flattening the lower corner into a triangle. Repeat on the right.

22) A: fold the flap up where shown, crease and unfold. B: Inside reverse the flap.

Step 19 is easier if your sink was made neatly. If not, try to encourage an octagonal shape as you flatten the paper.

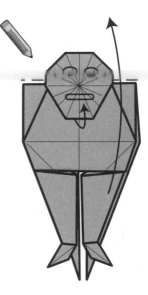

21) Add another scary face, then swing the lower half, including the head, upwards.

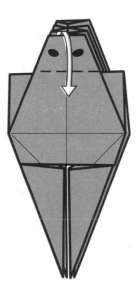

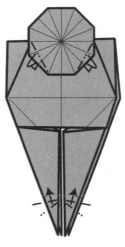

19) Carefully fold down the first edge, opening the paper into an octagon.

20) Shape the octagon with mountain folds, tucking them into pockets behind. Two small crimps form the feet.

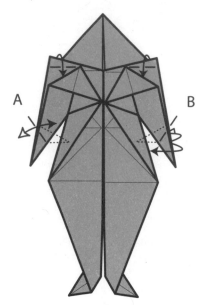

A   B

24) Fold two upper corners inside. Precrease and outside reverse the hands.

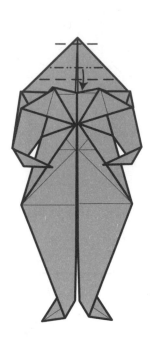

25) Make a pleat on the top flap, fold the upper corner down.

If you've reached this page, the folding is much easier!

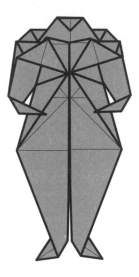

26) The model is complete. Turn the paper over.

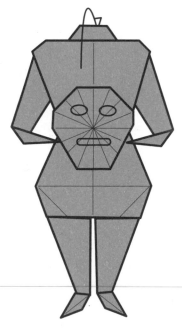

Here is the first horror subject, a headless man. Fold the top half of the body behind but keep the head in place.

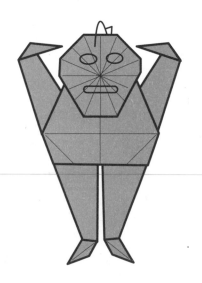

Here is the dwarf! Fold the head behind on the central hinge of paper to reveal the ghost!

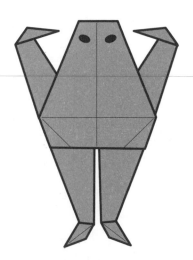

Tomb

Design by Nick Robinson

Lots of precreasing is required for this design. Try to be methodical and accurate as you add the folds. Remember to turn the paper over where indicated!

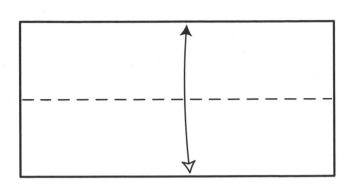

1) Start with half a square. Fold in half, crease and unfold.

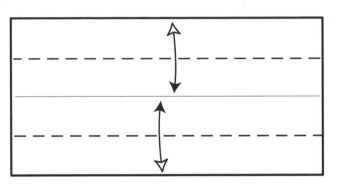

2) Fold upper and lower edges to the center, crease and unfold.

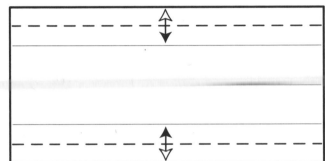

3) Crease the outer sections in half also, then turn over.

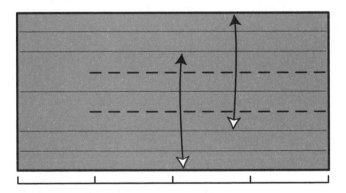

4) Fold upper and lower edges to the opposite 1/4 crease. Make the creases only in the right-hand 3/4 of the paper.

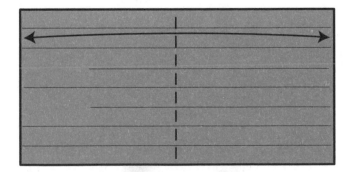

5) Fold in half from side to side, crease and unfold.

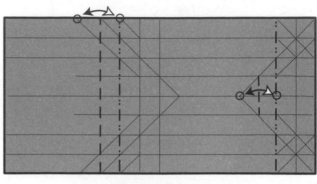

11) Fold (existing) creases as mountains to add new valley creases, then unfold.

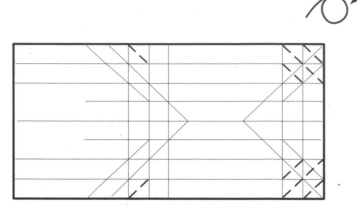

10) Yet more precreases please! Then turn the model over.

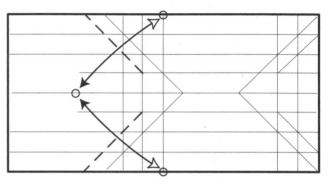

9) More precreases, made by joining the circled areas.

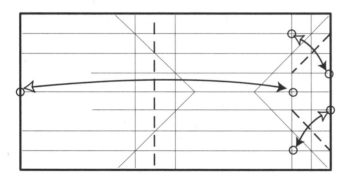

8) Fold the left edge to the circled area, crease and unfold. Add the small valley creases.

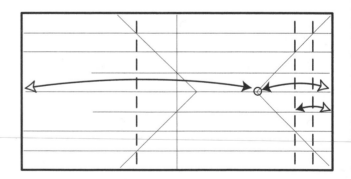

7) Fold right and left edges to the circled area, crease and unfold. Fold the right edge to the crease you've just made, then unfold.

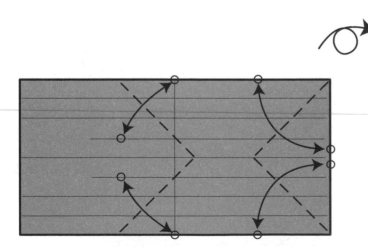

6) Make 45 degree creases where shown, by lining up the circled areas. Turn the model over.

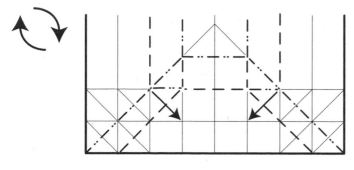

12) Rotate the paper and raise the paper into 3-D using the creases shown—check the next picture.

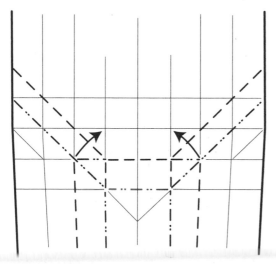

14) Unfold and make a similar move towards the other end of the paper. Refold the first end.

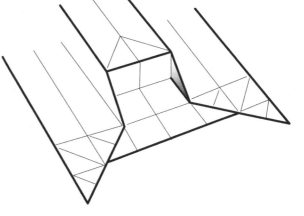

13) This is what you're aiming for. The paper is 3-D from one end to the other. Try not to add new creases.

When working with models that become 3-D during the folding sequence, it's sometimes easier to hold the paper in the air while folding. Be gentle with the paper.

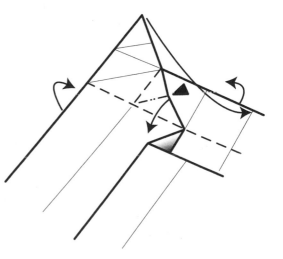

15) This is the result shown from a side-on view. Look in the direction indicated.

16) Raise the paper into 3-D using the creases shown.

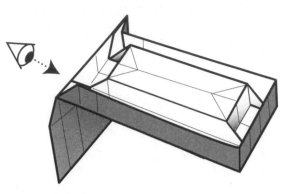

22) This is the result. Look from the direction shown.

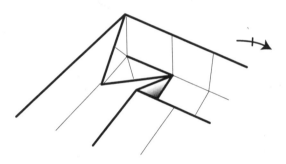

21) Rotate the paper. Lifting the sides, fold the end paper down.

20) This is the result. Repeat steps 16–19 on the nearby corner.

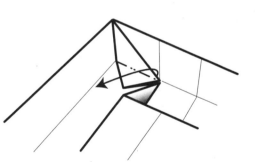

19) Unfold a flap.

Steps 17–20 need careful, calm folding. If you are struggling, use a larger square and fold only this corner, so you can work out what is happening.

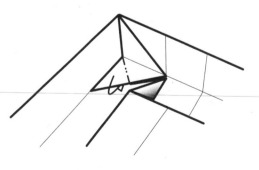

18) Carefully tuck the corner underneath.

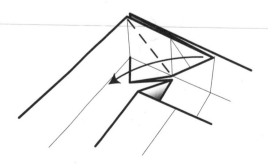

17) Fold the corner over.

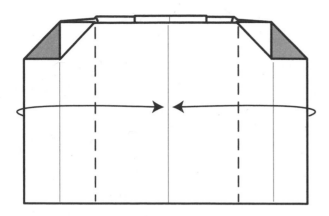

23) Fold the sides in to the center.

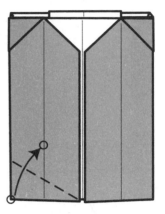

24) Fold the corner
to meet the crease.

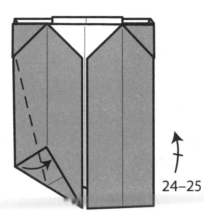

24–25

25) Fold the corner to lie
on the edge. Repeat
steps 24–25 on the right.

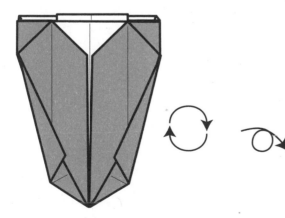

26) This is the result. Rotate
and turn the model over.

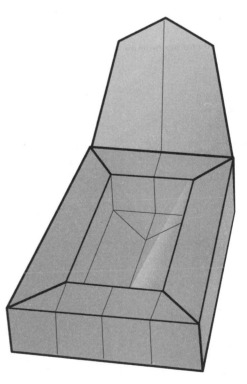

Vampire

Design by Nick Robinson

This is a design dating from the early 1980s when the author began to create origami designs. You'll find it easier to start with a larger square for the first attempt.

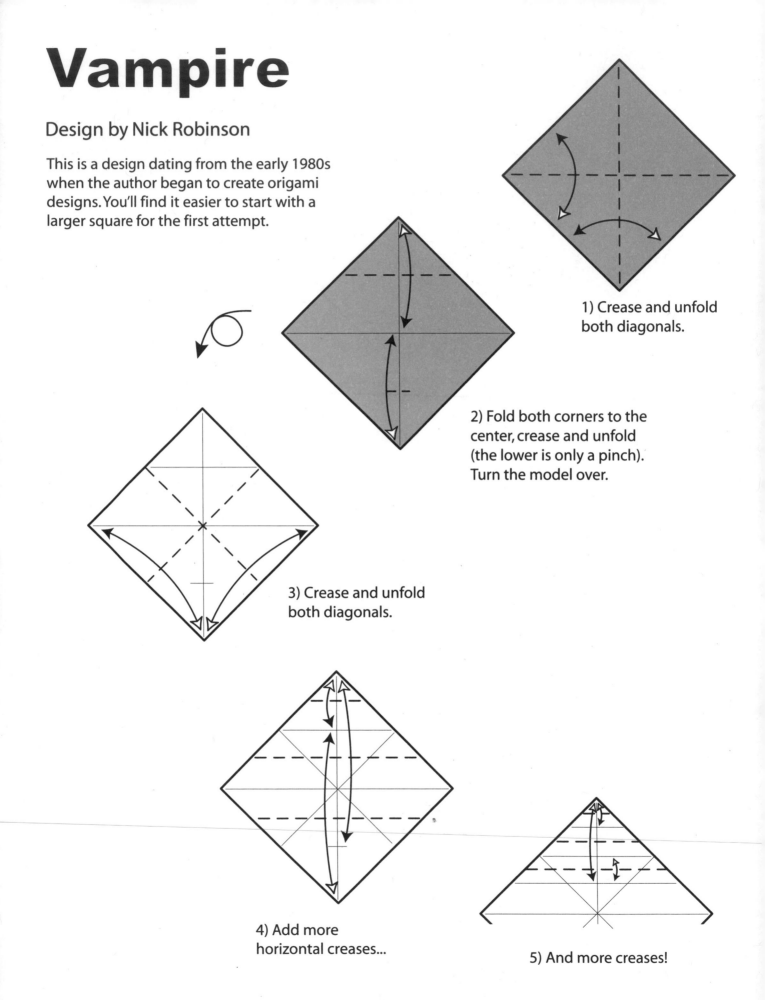

1) Crease and unfold both diagonals.

2) Fold both corners to the center, crease and unfold (the lower is only a pinch). Turn the model over.

3) Crease and unfold both diagonals.

4) Add more horizontal creases...

5) And more creases!

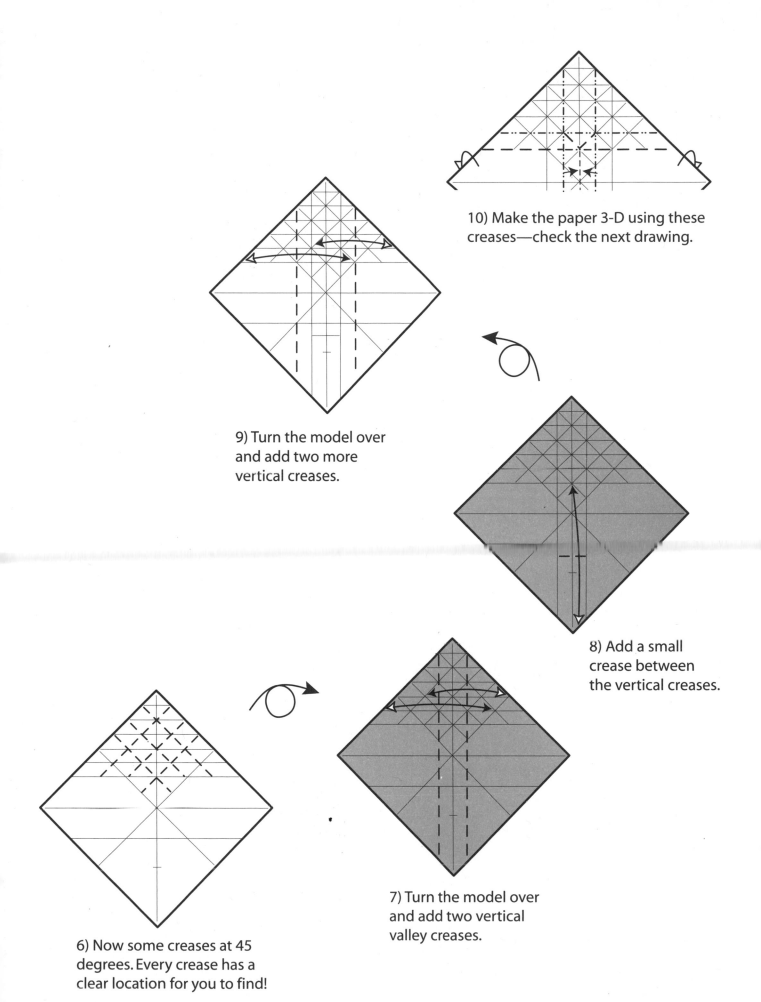

10) Make the paper 3-D using these creases—check the next drawing.

9) Turn the model over and add two more vertical creases.

8) Add a small crease between the vertical creases.

7) Turn the model over and add two vertical valley creases.

6) Now some creases at 45 degrees. Every crease has a clear location for you to find!

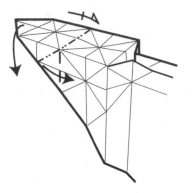

11) Form a square at the top using these creases.

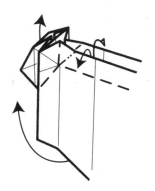

12) Sink the center of the square and flatten the side flaps.

This type of 3-D folding is always easier if you have sharp creases and the paper isn't too "tired." If it starts to lose shape, refold again from the start.

13) Use these creases to flatten the model once more.

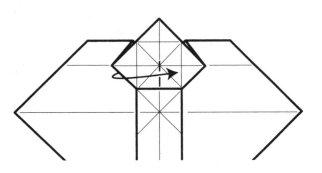

14) Lift up one side of the head to see the layers beneath.

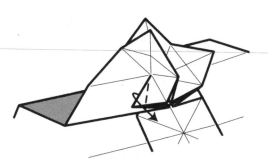

15) Fold the top left edge over, forming a small triangular point.

16) Fold over the point to form a fang—press firmly!

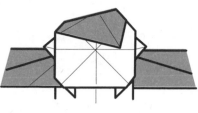

22) The head complete.

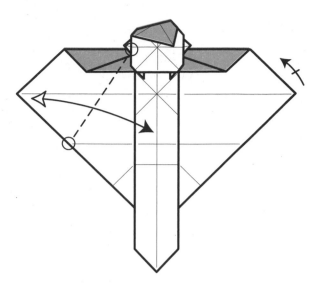

23) Make a crease between the circled points. Repeat on the right.

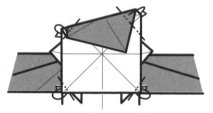

21) Shape the head to taste with mountain folds.

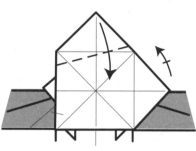

20) Fold the other ear to match the first. Fold the top corner down at an angle.

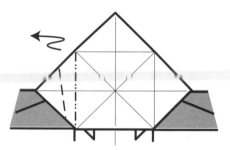

19) Fold the corner behind, then back out again to form an ear.

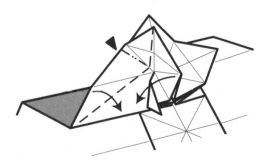

17) Fold the raw white edge to the folded edge. The shorter creases are slightly apart from existing creases and form themselves as you flatten the paper.

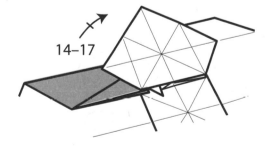

14–17

18) Repeat steps 14–17 on the right side.

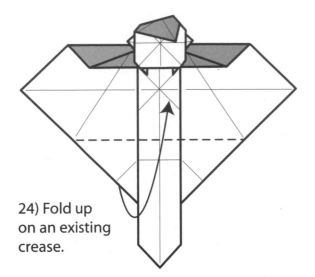

24) Fold up on an existing crease.

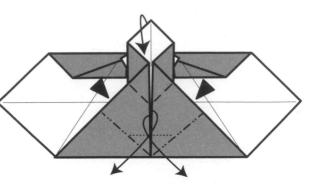

25) Open and squash the central section—the dotted line shows a hidden valley crease (see next drawing).

The final 3-D shaping of the model is something that you will need to practice to get right. You can have the arms overlapping slightly, or wider, to taste. Choosing slightly thicker paper may also help.

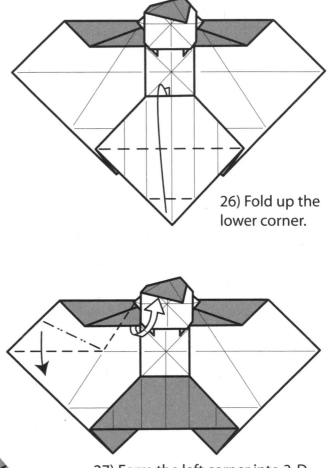

26) Fold up the lower corner.

27) Form the left corner into 3-D. Ease the head forwards by opening creases underneath it.

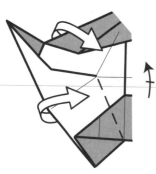

29) Make gentle valley creases to shape the body. Repeat steps 27–29 on the right.

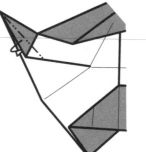

28) Fold the flap underneath to lock it.

Werewolf

Design by Nick Robinson

This is the most complex model in this book and so you may need to fold it several times to achieve a great result. Even so, is it far easier than many modern "ultra-complex" designs!

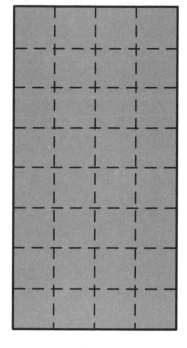

1) Start with a 2x1 rectangle. Crease into quarters one way and eighths the other.

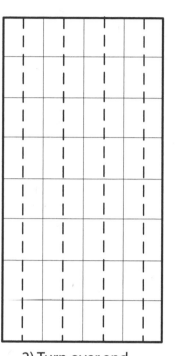

2) Turn over and add 1/8th creases.

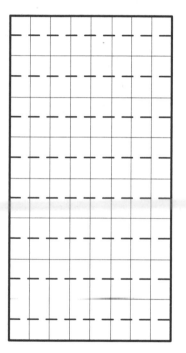

3) Add 1/16th creases.

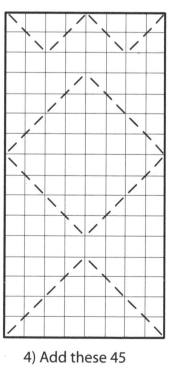

4) Add these 45 degree creases.

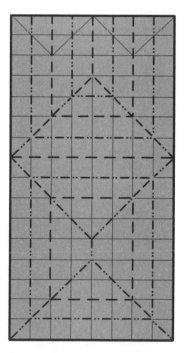

5) Turn over and begin to fold these creases.

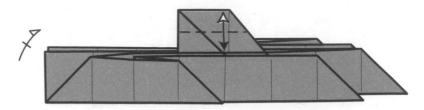

10) Repeat steps 8 to 9 on the rear left corner. Fold the top edge down, crease and unfold.

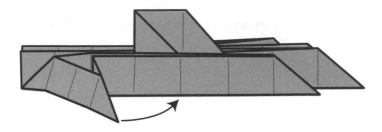

9) Fold the corner to the right.

The technique used here to create the base for the model is known as "box-pleating," invented in the 1960s by Neal Elias.

8) Start to press up a hidden edge as a mountain fold.

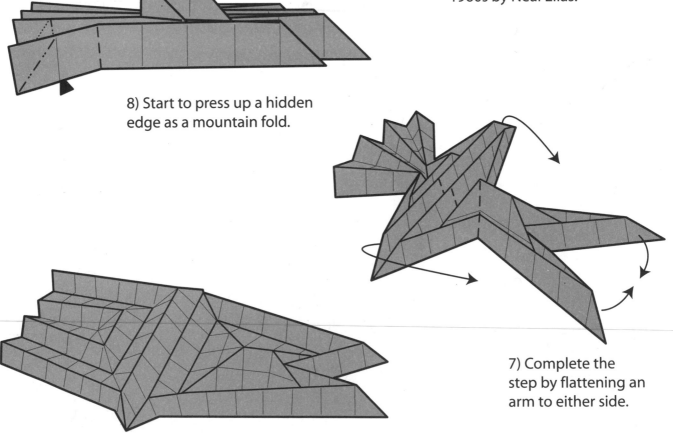

7) Complete the step by flattening an arm to either side.

6) The collapse in progress. Try not to force the paper.

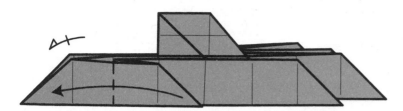

11) Fold a flap over to the left. Repeat behind.

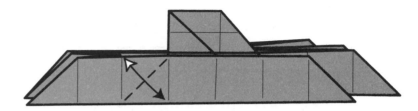

12) Make a firm crease through all layers, then unfold.

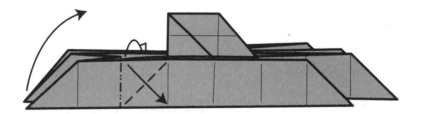

13) Make these creases on both sides at once, lifting up the corners on the left.

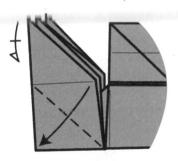

14) Fold down a single flap on either side. These will become the ears.

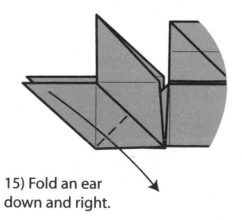

15) Fold an ear down and right.

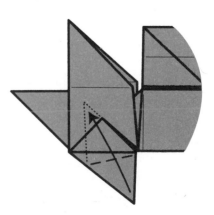

16) Fold the corner to the dotted line.

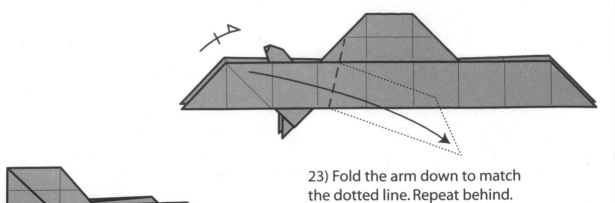

23) Fold the arm down to match the dotted line. Repeat behind.

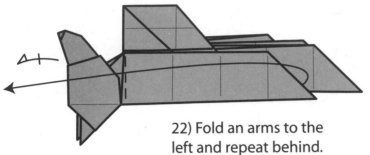

22) Fold an arms to the left and repeat behind.

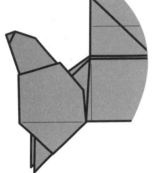

21) The head complete.

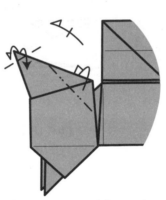

20) Wrap the nose outside and shape the jaw.

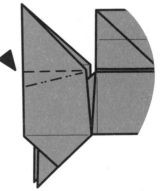

19) Precrease and crimp the nose inside.

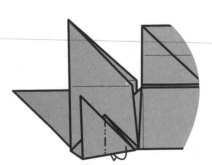

17) Fold the corner inside. There are several layers, so crease firmly.

15–18

18) Swing the ear down and repeat steps 15–18 on the other ear.

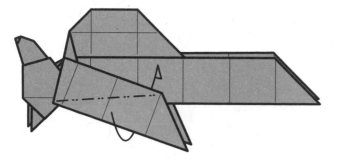

24) Wrap the arm underneath.

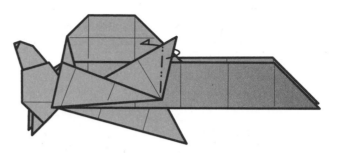

25) Fold the paw underneath.

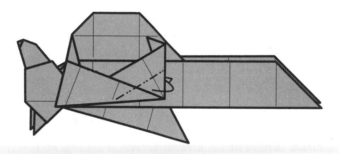

26) Fold part of the arm underneath.
There are several layers, so crease firmly.

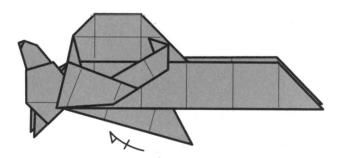

27) One arm is finished. Repeat
steps 24–26 on the other arm.

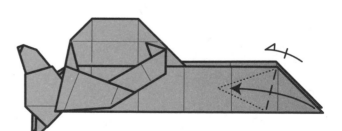

28) Fold a foot up to match the
dotted line. Repeat underneath.

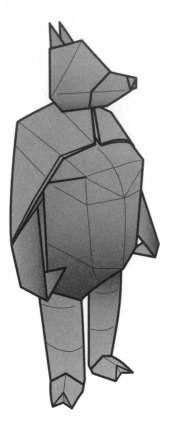

The 3-D shaping of the paper used here will need some practice to perfect. Try using slightly thicker paper and investigate "wet folding."

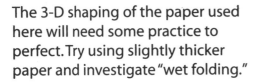

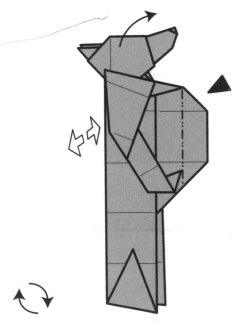

29) Rotate to this position. Open the body from the back and flatten the chest. Ease the head forwards.

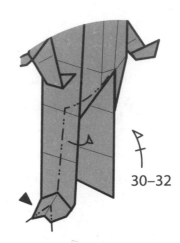

30–32

32) Push the end of the foot inside to suggest claws. Shape the leg and bring the foot slightly forwards. Repeat steps 30–32 on the other leg.

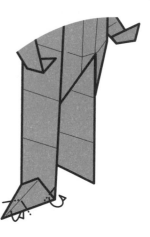

31) Fold the heel underneath (to help it stand) and wrap the end of the foot underneath.

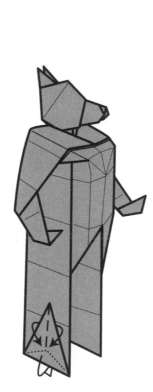

30) Make mountain folds on the dotted lines and pinch the foot together, to bring it forwards and down.

Acknowledgments

All models designed by Nick Robinson except: Fangs (Eric Kenneway), Vampire Mail (Francis Ow / Michel Grand), Trick or Treat? (Gilad Aharoni), Witches Brew (Simon Phillips / Tony Ayres), Cat's Head (David Petty), Finger Trap (Ilan Garibaldi), Horrors (Robert Neale), and Fright Mask (Nick Robinson / Wayne Brown).

The author would like to thank the staff at Dover who were involved in this book (M.C. Waldrep, Suzanne E. Johnson, and Marie Zaczkiewicz), the British Origami Society, Wayne Brown for valiant proofreading, and Himanshu Agrawal for support and encouragement. Lastly and most importantly, my wife Alison, children Nick and Daisy, and cats Rhubarb and Matilda for their love.

Please visit the author's website at *www.origami.me.uk*